Spirit Catcher

DATE DUE

DE 19 '98			
DE 16 '98			
AP 6 '99			
JE 10 '00			
DE 2 0 '00			
DE 10 '01			
AP 1 2 '04			
NO 15 '05			

DEMCO 38-296

Spirit Catcher

The Life and Art of John Coltrane

John Fraim

GREATHOUSE

ISBN 0-9645561-0-3
LCCN 95-75444

Published by
The GreatHouse Company
167 Oak Drive
West Liberty, Ohio 43357
513-465-5400
513-465-5401 (FAX)

The GreatHouse Company publishes books which explore unique and
provocative aspects of contemporary culture and thought. To be put on
the GreatHouse mailing list, or, for information on future GreatHouse
books contact the publisher at the above address.

Cover and interior design by Lightbourne Images
Original cover painting by Teresa Long
Editing by Custom Editorial Productions
Distributed to the Trade by Atrium Publishers Group

ATTENTION RETAILERS, COLLEGES AND UNIVERSITIES, CORPOR-
ATIONS, ORGANIZATIONS AND ASSOCIATIONS: Quantity dis-
counts are available on bulk purchases of this book. For information
contact Atrium Publishers Group, 3356 Coffey Lane, Santa Rosa, CA
95403, 800-275-2606

Spirit Catcher

Table of Contents

"During the year 1957, I experienced by the grace of God, a spiritual awakening which was to lead me to a richer, fuller, more productive life. At that time, in gratitude, I humbly asked to be given the means and privilege to make others happy through music. I feel this has been granted through His grace."

John Coltrane

Part One
Disciple

Twilight

I f you have ever experienced a tropical storm, you know the strange portents of its arrival: trees pushed into wild contortions by heavy, thick air; birds darting about; large dark clouds rolling like mountains on gigantic wheels, while all around the atmosphere takes on a yellowish egg yolk color.

During the fifties I spent some years in Florida and these storm images are still sharply remembered. We lived in a small house close to the Atlantic, and as the storms approached I would often walk out onto the beach and stand against the strong, warm wind and watch the ocean. Waves fifteen feet high assaulted the beach in magnificent foamy explosions, like advance forces. And in the distance of the great raging body of water, the yellowish agitated sky mixed with the dark ocean, a massive watercolor painting continually in the process of creation, heaven and earth welded, making it impossible to discern the horizon.

The mass of welded atmosphere, constantly exploding into new shapes and patterns, whirled like a giant top on the verge of collapsing. Jagged white thunderbolts briefly illuminated the darkness of the approaching storm.

Today these images still come to mind. It is early

December in the Bay Area and the sky is a brilliant, clear blue. The chill air feels as if thousands of tiny daggers are constantly pricking your skin. Under the clear sun everything sparkles and there is a certain eternal quality to life. The cool air brings a stillness and peacefulness.

However, the weather is strangely reminiscent of Florida in the fifties and the arrival of the great tropical storms. It's both dangerous and exciting, and these two qualities constantly push like the welded mass of earth and sky from the tropical storms. In this environment life's horizons and boundaries become difficult to discern.

It is a twilight time when one age is dying and a new age is yet to be born. There is an atmosphere of anticipation in this peculiar transitional period, and even when the air is clear and cool you can sometimes briefly feel this tropical storm atmosphere. It is an internal, psychic weather having little to do with the real weather.

My radio, tuned to the local jazz station out of Berkeley, plays mellow jazz this Sunday afternoon. I half-listen as I lazily go about Sunday chores around the house. Much of it is homogenized elevator Musak which dominates the pop airwaves. The contemporary jazz trend attempts to blend rock and jazz but the resulting creation is an odd orphan rather than a strong new music.

Like many members of my generation I gauge the climate of the times by the music created. Once the music meant something but now that time is past. Now it seems forced on us solely for the profit of record companies.

When the work around the house is finished, evening

falls and lights of houses twinkle in the hills beneath my home in the East Bay. I plan to drive into Berkeley for dinner, but as I reach to turn off the radio a familiar gong announces the beginning of John Coltrane's *A Love Supreme* album. I turn up the volume and sit on the porch overlooking the homes below and the hazy lights of San Francisco across the bay. Coltrane gets little play over the airwaves, and only a venturesome disc jockey dares play his music.

Listening to the music I again realize what music has meant to me. In the twilight of another day, another period of history, I think about John Coltrane and his arrival on the jazz scene in the forties. It was pervaded by an atmosphere similar to those times in Florida I remember before the great tropical storms. And it was a time much like today when one era was dying and another being born.

When Coltrane appeared on the jazz scene in the mid-forties, the music had worked itself into a peculiar corner. With roots largely in a spontaneous oral tradition, it had evolved into complex composed music written for and played by large orchestras. In this evolution, it had traveled a long way from New Orleans and the music of Jelly Roll Morton and Louis Armstrong. Somewhere along the journey it had metamorphosed into an entirely new music which called itself jazz but was really the popular music of the time.

Whatever the case, the music had lost much of the original power it once possessed because the improvisational element of jazz had to be toned down in the large orchestral context. In those early years, the musicians would dance and shake as they played their instruments, so that it often looked as if they were plugged into a strong electrical current. The music was jagged and often incomplete, but there was growth in it. And there was a great joy by many who played it for being able to partake in this growth process. Musicians now sat behind their individual little bandstands, six or seven to a row, three rows deep. They wore suits and remained seated unless they soloed. Improvisation was now relegated to these solos, confined to an agreed-on number of bars held tightly within the compositional framework.

The music became another victim of the American love of size. "The bigger the better" was the contemporary rallying cry of the American economic system during these wartime years, and there was no limit to what a highly organized system of mass production could accomplish. Jazz had become a factor of the economic system and, although a relatively small one, its style and context were greatly influenced by the larger system. This connection with the general populace was, during the forties, the strongest it has ever been.

Jazz was big business in the arts, and being a jazz musician in those years was like being an employee of a large corporation. Every member of those large orchestras had certain functions to perform as they sat on the stages of large ballrooms with hundreds of people dancing in front of them. And, as in large corporations, these functions left little room for individual creativity or spontaneous musical thoughts.

More than most art forms, the history of jazz reflected that great battle mankind wages against the forces of order and chaos. Jazz had always had its great improvisers, such as Armstrong, and its great composers, such as Ellington—its own forces of chaos and order. Until the forties these extremes were able to exist together in a symbiotic relationship. One extreme never threatened to totally obliterate the other and, more often than not, mutual growth resulted from the exchange of ideas.

The forties, though, saw order and composition increasingly dominate the improvisational, spontaneous forms. For the first time, the historical tension of the music seemed to break as the large structured orchestras gobbled up all the promising young improvisers. For the first time, the spontaneous expression of the individual musician was seriously threatened. As is true with large corporations, it was impossible to run a large orchestra without certain well-defined rules and procedures.

Some saw the problem and realized that the music must be given back to the improvisers for it to grow again. To them, jazz had flowed into an artistic backwater where continued growth was increasingly difficult. They felt its continued growth must come from small jazz combos.

Musicians such as Thelonious Monk, Kenny Clarke, Charlie Christian, Dizzy Gillespie and Charlie Parker began meeting in places like New York's Minton's and developing music for small jazz groups. Unlike compositions for large orchestras, this music usually lacked strong melody. When melody did appear in the music, it was often in quick melodic fragments. Unlike orchestral jazz, quarter notes no longer dominated but were replaced with eighth notes. Critics commented that the sounds characteristic of the music were "racing, nervous phrases." It was almost impossible to play this music in large orchestras.

This new jazz was "bebop" and Charlie Parker became its leader. When Parker blew his saxophone, notes danced out in such quick succession that listeners could seldom maintain their musical bearings. Parker chopped up the old rhythms and time signatures and juxtaposed them in new, unique ways so the listener was often startled by having heard something truly for the first (and usually last) time. Parker never had the answers in that saxophone—only more and more questions. He showed other musicians that one phrase did not necessarily have to follow another, that each phrase had a number of possibilities expanding from it. More than anything else, though, he laid a foundation for a contemporary return to the original concerns and strengths of music, a return which could incorporate the melodic and rhythmic sophistication of large swing bands into small jazz groups.

During this time a young saxophone player named John Coltrane appeared on the jazz scene. He was well prepared for the task at hand.

Apprenticeship

He was born in Hamlet, North Carolina, on September 23, 1926, a day with important astrological significance. As Bill Cole notes in his book *John Coltrane*, "His birth was on the day of the autumn equinox, on the cusp of Virgo and Libra, one of the two days during the year in which night and day are in perfect balance." Later, Coltrane would acknowledge the importance of astrology in his life with such pieces as "Fifth House" (1959), "Equinox" (1960), "Crescent" (1964), and "Cosmos" (1965).

Two months after his birth, his family moved one hundred miles away to High Point, North Carolina, where he lived in a two-story frame house on top of a hill in the "good" black section of town with his parents, his aunt and uncle and their daughter Mary, and his grandparents, the Blairs. The Reverend Blair was a powerful, dynamic minister of the African Methodist Episcopal Zion Church and had once been a state senator representing the area around Edenton, North Carolina. His father, John Robert Coltrane, ran his own tailor shop but his real love was music. C.O. Simpkins writes about Coltrane's father in *Coltrane, A Biography*, saying that "Sometimes he would prop up his feet, get a couple of shots of whiskey in him...and sing country music for hours, playing the violin or ukulele he had taught himself." His mother also loved music and had wanted to pursue a career as an opera singer. Unfortunately this was not possible and so she sang and played the piano in the church choir.

On Sundays, young Coltrane would sit in a straight-backed wooden pew inside the small brick church and listen to his grandfather preach. The Reverend Blair was known throughout the state for his charismatic personality and strong leadership. C.O. Simpkins writes that the reverend "could set the people on fire—make them shout, make them weep, make them thunder the floor with stomping feet." Then he, continues Simpkins, "talked about them, told of their sins and gossip, while always preserving their clinging hope of sustaining any hardship." Typical of Methodist and Baptist churches, the service involved a powerful interaction between the minister and the congregation, and Reverend Blair was one of the best at evoking strong, emotional responses. Intermixed with the preaching in his grandfather's church was music, often the music born out of the suffering of the black people in the South, a music called spirituals—an extended scream of agony, a primal scream, a twisting, moaning cry of pain—all these elements and more placed within musical notes and sung, on those Sunday mornings throughout the 1930s, in that little brick church in High Point, North Carolina.

When he was older Coltrane would go to the church on

Tuesday evenings. There, the Reverend Warren Steele would conduct the rehearsals for the Community Band. In *Chasin' The Trane*, J.C. Thomas notes that the reverend was a musician himself "who rather single-handedly decided that what the black community of High Point most needed at that moment, with the ominous vibrations of World War II rapidly approaching, was some music of character and quality." Young Coltrane played his first musical instrument in this band—an alto saxophone.

The initial success of Reverend Steele's Community Band led some of its members to put together a band at William Penn High School. Coltrane was one of them. The band practiced twice a week, on Tuesdays and Thursdays, in the high school auditorium. At first Coltrane played clarinet, but changed to the alto saxophone in his senior year.

During this time music began to increasingly dominate his life. Around 1940 he started reading the jazz magazine *Down Beat*. His neighbors could often hear him at three or four in the morning practicing his horn in the backyard. He was known as *the* musician in the band and students would seek him out at school and ask him for musical advice.

In the early forties white big bands dominated the charts, and Coltrane usually heard bands such as the Dorsey Brothers, Harry James and Glenn Miller. Less frequently he heard the bands of Duke Ellington and Count Basie. However, musicians in the Ellington and Basie bands were his first major influences.

The Count Basie band had the celebrated tenor soloist

Lester Young, who would soon become one of the most important musicians in the history of jazz. Lester Young was the first true musical influence on Coltrane. In contrast to the other great tenor saxophonist of the time, Coleman Hawkins, Young's sound was more introverted and lyrical. As critic Joachim Berendt notes, Young had a "cautious tone, friendly and obliging on fast pieces, full of tender abandon on slow numbers, reserved in utterance, never stating a nuance more than absolutely necessary." During these early years with Count Basie, Young was creating some of the most important work of his career, such as "Lady Be Good," "Shoe Shine Boy,""Boogie Woogie" and "Evenin'." Many critics agree that his solos on these pieces rank with the finest in jazz—and Coltrane was listening to them during his formative years.

It is not surprising that Coltrane wanted a tenor saxophone so he could sound like Lester Young. Reverend Steele, though, felt that an alto saxophone would be easier for a youngster to handle. Coltrane followed his advice and started playing the alto horn. When this happened his new idol became the popular soloist in the Ellington orchestra, Johnny Hodges. The major influence for Hodges was Sidney Bechet. Hodges had a warm, subtle vibrato and was one of the greatest soloists in the Ellington bands.

In 1939, when Coltrane was thirteen, a number of tragedies struck his family. First, his father died. This was closely followed by Reverend Blair's death and, soon after this, his uncle's death. The sudden deaths of the important men in his life left a deep impression on young Coltrane and later greatly influenced his music, especially the music of the sixties. Growing up in a fairly well-to-do black family, Coltrane had never suffered or "paid his dues" like many other black youngsters. He had listened to the spirituals in church and had heard his grandfather's preaching, but in many ways it must have been difficult for him to really feel the pain and suffering, the emotion. With these deaths, he paid some dues early and began to see existence spiritually.

With the death of the men in the family, his mother was forced to find employment. Work was hard to find in High Point during those years, but she was able to find a job at the white country club in High Point. In a few years, though, she decided to leave High Point for Philadelphia, where work was more lucrative. In 1943, after graduating from high school, her son did the same thing.

Arriving in Philadelphia in June of 1943, Coltrane found accommodations in a small one-room apartment and employment as a laborer in a sugar-refining factory. A few months later, he was accepted as a student at the Ornstein School of Music—one of the better music schools in the city. The founder of the school, Leo Ornstein, was a pianist who had once studied under the famous Paderewski. Coltrane's teacher at Ornstein was Mike Guerra, a middle-aged man who had played sax in Philadelphia section bands for many years. In J.C. Thomas' book, Guerra states that Coltrane was easily the best student in his class. "I wrote out complex chord progressions," Guerra says, "and special exercises in chromatic scales, and he was one of the few who brought his homework back practically the next day and played it on sight. It was amazing the way he absorbed everything I gave him. He was always asking for more." Coltrane studied with Guerra for about a year while working in the sugar refinery.

During these early Philadelphia years, he started playing in some of the small cocktail bars around town. Thomas notes that Philadelphia was studded with these corner bars at the time. They featured small combos which played mostly for food and primarily to work out their musical ideas in public.

In 1945 Coltrane was drafted into the Navy and sent off to one of the Hawaiian islands, where he spent a year playing clarinet in a band called the Melody Makers. When he returned to Philadelphia in 1946, the big band swing music he had grown up listening to was under full attack from Charlie Parker and the new music called bebop. With all those years of constant practice in High Point behind him, possessing a powerful inner strength from being raised in a deeply religious family, and with a foundation in musical theory and an innate curiosity about life, Coltrane was well prepared to seriously enter the battle.

He found a small one-room apartment in the heart of Philadelphia's North Side ghetto. In the apartment there was a cot, a record player and one picture—that of Charlie Parker. In this small apartment he practiced his music all day and late into the night. When he was not practicing, he spent his time playing at some of the small neighborhood bars with his two good friends, Bill Barron and Benny Golson. When they could, they would catch tenor man Jimmy Oliver at one of the clubs around town. As Thomas notes, Oliver's "fingering was almost as fast as a submachine gun on automatic fire, and John was thinking about increasing his ability to play fast."

During this period he was hearing and playing more rhythm and blues than anything else and soon began landing jobs in some fairly well-known R&B bands. He played with Joe Webb at first, and then King Kolax. In 1947, Eddie "Cleanhead" Vinson heard Coltrane practicing at the musicians' union hall and asked him to join his band. Vinson, a primitive blues man from Texas, was searching for someone who could sound like Parker. Coltrane joined Vinson and toured with him cross-country for a little over a year. While with Vinson, he switched from an alto to a tenor sax and this change, Coltrane later remarked, "opened a wider area of listening" for him because no one dominated the tenor like Parker dominated the alto. As his musical interests expanded, he drew from all the people he heard on tenor, particularly the melodic phrasing of Lester Young and the arpeggios of Coleman Hawkins.

In late 1947, while the Vinson band was playing an extended engagement in California, a momentous meeting occurred. Charlie Parker, recently released from the state mental institution at Camarillo, where he had been confined for a nervous breakdown, was trying to revive his music. He would often appear for impromptu sessions at the Los Angeles home of bassist Red Callender, only a few blocks from the ocean. Pianist Erroll Garner, then staying with Callender, and Parker would often join them in informal sessions.

One Sunday afternoon Coltrane, who had heard about these sessions, hitched a ride out to Callender's place and played with Parker for the first time. It was not their first meeting. A year earlier, Coltrane had briefly met Parker backstage after a performance at Philadelphia's Academy of Music. But it was the first time that the two really had a chance to talk and exchange musical ideas. During their discussion, Parker showed the young Coltrane how to play a piece he had recently written—which he had been playing that day—about his Camarillo experience. It was called "Relaxin' at Camarillo" and would become one of Parker's most important works.

Leaving the Vinson band around June of 1948, Coltrane picked up a number of smaller gigs with lesser-known bands. He played out the remainder of 1948 with two of these lesser-known bands, the Heath Brothers band and the Howard McGhee band. In the McGhee band he played one of the two alto saxophone chairs, with Jimmy Heath playing the other, and traveled with the band to engagements in New York and Chicago. When the band returned to New York, McGhee cut the band to a sextet. Heath was kept on but Coltrane was let go.

For the first time in almost two years, he was out of a job and was forced to return to the Philadelphia cocktail circuit and play one-night gigs in places where drinking was a lot more important than music. A tradition in many of these small clubs at the time, called "walking the bar," required the musician to walk on top of the bar while playing his instrument. Coltrane was forced to walk the bar in many of these clubs. To any serious musician, it was an incredibly humiliating experience—to someone like Coltrane, who was developing a type of religious fervor for his music, it was devastating.

In addition to the humiliation of being forced to walk the bar, Coltrane's music was under attack from both audiences and club owners as being too "far out." Even musicians found him hard to understand, and when Coltrane went to Greensboro, North Carolina, during this time for a short gig, the musicians dreaded to see him come; many of them felt he couldn't play.

Faced with these frustrations, music began to seem like a dead-end street and he became deeply depressed. In his depression he acquired a habit that would remain with him through much of his life: heroin. The drug was very prevalent among musicians at this time and was readily obtainable in the black neighborhoods. In the thirties gin and marijuana were fashionable. But in the forties the more debilitating heroin was the major vice. And in an effort to cut down on his use of heroin, Coltrane acquired another vice—alcohol. Nat Hentoff in *Jazz Is* remembers seeing Coltrane one evening in the early fifties in Greenwich Village with a bottle of wine in his hand. As Hentoff remembers, "He looked awful. Raggedy, vacant."

The times were not all bad for Coltrane, though. Intermixed with his depression and the beginning of a drug habit were some events which would have a major impact on his life. One was the growing friendship with the trumpeter and composer Calvin "Folks" Massey. The two had first met in the Heath band and had quickly became friends. Their musical ideas were often the same and both had a growing curiosity about life. They would make frequent trips to the library to read all types of books and they would spend much time listening to European composers such as Bartok and Stravinsky. Massey, Simpkins relates, would often steal the scores. One day he ran into Coltrane's apartment with a stolen copy of Stravinsky's "Firebird Suite," and in reading it they came across many interesting musical concepts. One of these was the use of the double diminished scale which, when played, gives the feeling of falling uncontrollably downward. As Simpkins notes, "John played the scale backwards, forward, testing numerous variations" and "added it to his growing body of ideas." This friendship would continue throughout Coltrane's life; Massey would read Coltrane's poem from *A Love Supreme* at Coltrane's funeral.

If heroin was debilitating many black musicians at this time, a rising positive force which counteracted the effects of this drug was the Islamic religion. During the mid-forties, musicians such as Art Blakey and Ahmad Jamal raised money to bring Moslem teachers to America. Philadelphia was one of the major places where the religion began to take hold, and Coltrane was exposed to it largely through his friendship with a huge, bald-headed black Moslem he met in 1949, Yusef Lateef. Their friendship began at the start of Coltrane's first apprenticeship, when he joined the Dizzy Gillespie band. Although Lateef was only briefly in Gillespie's band, he aroused in Coltrane a latent interest in religion and philosophy. The big saxophonist suggested that Coltrane read works such as the Koran, and authors such as Kahlil Gibran and Jiddu Krishnamurti. He also loaned him books from his own collection of Eastern works. This was the beginning of Coltrane's interest in Eastern philosophy, which found musical expression during the sixties.

Playing with Gillespie was a very important event in Coltrane's career and helped put his life back on track. Along with Parker, Gillespie was the major architect of the bebop movement, and from the early forties the two were inseparable. In 1943 they played together in Earl Hines' band; in 1944 they played with Billy Eckstine, and later both led combos on 52nd Street in New York.

The combination was unique. Parker, the tortured, introverted genius, was the great creator of bebop who never developed the ability to sell himself and his music. Gillespie, on the other hand, was the great international salesman of bebop music. As Joachim Berendt notes in *The Jazz Book*, "If he did not bring to this music the creative impulses that radiated from Charlie Parker, he gave it the glamour and power without which it could not have conquered the world." Billy Eckstein further observed that whereas Parker was responsible for the actual playing of bebop more than anyone else, Gillespie was responsible for putting it down.

In addition to being the great salesman and preserver of bebop music, Gillespie was also a master musician from whom Coltrane learned a great deal. As Coltrane later recalled, "I was first awakened to musical exploration by Diz and Bird. It was through their music that I began to learn about musical structure and the more theoretical aspects of music." Eckstein once related that Gillespie was "one of the smartest guys around. Musically, he knew what he was doing backwards and forwards."

One of the things under attack from Gillespie and Parker was the traditional quarter and eighth note time signature serving as the structure for much of composed, orchestral jazz. Leonard Feather remarks in *The Jazz Book*, "Where earlier trumpeters had expressed themselves, say, mainly in eighth notes...Gillespie was able, through an unprecedented alliance of imagination and technique, to unleash a glittering waterfall of sixteenth notes, simultaneously implying, through his choice of notes, a more complex harmonic structure."

For Coltrane, struggling to get his music together once again, the awakening experience with Gillespie was a shock at first. By his admission, he was playing "clichés" and "hip" tunes when he first entered Gillespie's band and needed to learn how to express his unique musical personality.

Musical expression, though, was hampered by Coltrane's increasing addiction to heroin. Once, while on tour with the band, he passed out in a hotel room and was revived by fellow band member Jimmy Heath through mouth-to-mouth resuscitation. On the road in California, he pawned his watch to get money for drugs. More often than not, he would appear late for gigs. In Canada, while the band was on a brief tour, he missed a show and Gillespie was forced to fire him.

The Gillespie apprenticeship lasted two years. During this time, Coltrane is first heard on record with the November 21, 1949, performance on *Dizzy Gillespie And His Orchestra*. His second, and final, record date with Gillespie was March 1, 1951, and is on the album *Dizzy Gillespie Sextet*. When he returned to Philadelphia in 1951, he worked with bands of questionable quality, playing everything from rock 'n' roll to polka—once—in upstate New York.

While these short engagements did not add much to his musical credentials, they did give him time to pursue peripheral matters: time for intense practice and study, and time to further consolidate his increasingly evident musical abilities. And, too, he wanted to make the big switch from alto to tenor sax, on which he could really be original.

He applied to the Granoff School of Music and, upon the recommendations of former students Dizzy Gillespie and Percy Heath, was soon accepted. Founded in 1918 by the Russian violinist Isadore Granoff, the school was one of the country's foremost institutions of the modern composer, Stravinsky. Granoff had performed at the Paris premiere of Stravinsky's "Le Sacre du Printemps" in 1913.

At Granoff, Coltrane's music theory teacher, Dennis Sandole, and his saxophone instructor, Matthew Rastelli, were extremely knowledgeable musicians and demanding teachers. And both realized the incredible potential of their student. Rastelli is quoted by Thomas as saying that, "Coltrane was so far out in his ideas and techniques that every time I heard him practicing, I'd stop and listen." It was Sandole, though, who would have a great influence on Coltrane's music. He persuaded Coltrane to listen to classical music of the modern masters such as Debussy, Ravel, Bartok and Stravinsky. He once told Sandole that Debussy's "Le Mer" gave him the feeling of swimming in a sea of instruments. Coltrane began spending hours and hours listening to these composers and came to admire Stravinsky the most, but it was Bartok that he listened to and enjoyed the most.

Coltrane spent his weekdays at Granoff and picked up gigs in the evenings and on weekends. When he was not studying or playing he spent most of his time reading and attempting to satisfy his growing philosophical curiosity about life. It was an inborn curiosity to a certain extent, but one that had also developed from events from his early life such as his religious upbringing, the early deaths of the most important men in his life, and friendships with people like Calvin Massey and Yusef Lateef. It was a curiosity also nurtured by the unique musical education he was receiving both on the road with well-known bands and at home in places like the Ornstein and Granoff music schools.

However, for Coltrane in these years there never seemed to be a balance between philosophy and music, between an expanding education and application of this education in a musical context. The swings back and forth between the two extremes led to a concentration on one at the expense of the other. Playing with a well-known band like Gillespie's took a time commitment which left little time for study or reflection. And study and education left little time to practice his music. For Coltrane, who was becoming a philosopher almost as much as a musician, the extremes were always there and the balance between them remained elusive.

In the early 1950s, Coltrane's focus on education forced him into cheap clubs. Clubs like the Cafe Society, Joe Pitt's Musical Bar and the Zanzibar in Philadelphia at this time offered cheap musical contexts where club owners and patrons demanded entertainment from the musicians as much as music. In clubs such as these Coltrane was forced to walk the bar again and make unusual "honking" sounds with his horn. Going to school and studying philosophy and consolidating musical skills took some money, and clubs like these seemed to be the only real source of this money.

From 1952 through 1954, though, the great pendulum of his life swung the other way and he once again returned to the road to practice his art under the tutelage of two old jazz masters from the thirties whom he had admired for many years. Their names were Earl Bostic and Johnny Hodges.

Joining the Earl Bostic band in 1952, Coltrane under-took an apprenticeship under a master technician of the art. As Art Blakey once said, "If Coltrane played with Bostic, I know he learned a lot. Nobody knew more about the saxophone than Bostic, I mean technically, and that includes Bird." Then Blakey added, "Working with Bostic is like attending a university of the saxophone." Bostic's saxophone was rough-edged and hard-toned and was one of the few sounds on the scene at the time which was not under the Parker spell. Born in Tulsa, Oklahoma, in 1913, Bostic had worked in Harlem in 1941 with Hot Lips Page, and in 1943 had joined the legendary Lionel Hampton. More than anything else, Coltrane learned about fingering techniques from Bostic. He also started the break from Parker while with Bostic.

Leaving Bostic, he joined the Johnny Hodges band in 1953. From the experience of working with a master technician, he went into the experience of working with a master stylist. Hodges, the old idol of Coltrane when he was in High Point, had been the major alto sax stylist before Parker. His style of stretching, lingering over and caressing notes was the antithesis of the quick, jabbing Parker style and would later be responsible for the beautiful lyricism in Coltrane's music during the late fifties and early sixties. More than anything else, he learned intonation from Hodges. Years later Coltrane remembered that they played "honest" music in the Hodges band and that it was his "education to the older generation." He continues, noting that, "I really enjoyed that job...Nothing was superficial. It all had meaning and it all swung...Besides enjoying my stay with Johnny musically, I also enjoyed it because I was getting firsthand information about things that happened way before my time."

The ever-present extreme in his life through all of these

back-and-forth swings, though, was addiction to alcohol and heroin. Unlike the swings in his life between learning and playing music, it only went one way—it only got worse. Hodges' bassist John Williams recalls that "Coltrane would be sitting in his chair, holding his horn but not moving his fingers, the sax still in his mouth but not playing. It was obvious that he was using drugs." And in the end Hodges, who loved Coltrane almost as a son, was forced to let him go in the fall of 1954.

At this time Coltrane's career reached its lowest point. It was back to walking the bar and backing flashy acts such as Bull Moose Jackson, Big Maybelle, and Daisy Mae and the Hepcats. He seemed available for any type of band where a little work would put food on the table and dope in his arm. Working with Daisy Mae was like working with an early version of Ike and Tina Turner. Pianist Bill Evans comments about them that "This was the kind of band you'd find in Las Vegas lounges ten years later. Daisy Mae would shimmy out front in a sparkling dress while her husband, the guitar player, was boogying behind her."

During this period, when this extreme addiction seemed to dominate his life, when Coltrane was playing at places which often embarrassed old friends who came to see him, a great positive force entered his life. Her name was Naima and she was a Moslem. She was also a mother of a fatherless five-year-old daughter named Syeeda.

In June of 1954 he first met her at a cocktail party at the house of fellow musician Steve Davis. The two had much in common. Naima came from a musical family and was very involved in music. Her brothers were the jazz musicians Earl and Carl Grubbs. During her childhood she had been exposed to the music of Bartok and she was involved in astrology.

More than anything or anyone else, Naima was able to help Coltrane collect all the scattered pieces and mediate the extremes in his life. In helping him do this she also prepared him for the last and most important apprenticeships in his life: those with Miles Davis and Thelonious Monk. For when he left Monk in 1957 he never had to walk the bar again. He was his own man for the first time in his life.

Awakening

While bop's quick, jagged phrases made it the major jazz innovation of the forties, there was another style in embryonic form during these years. Lester Young, Coltrane's old idol, spent the thirties and forties developing a style which was almost a musical antithesis to that of Parker. In contrast to the turbulent and seldom melodic sound of bop, Young pioneered the use of longer phrases which eventually pushed jazz toward a new calmness and smoothness, a "modesty in musical expression" as Andre Hodier notes. This style eventually came to be called "cool jazz" to separate it from the raging, excited phrases of hot bebop jazz.

By the mid-forties, cool jazz had reached the height of its popularity. But in its ascension it had divided jazz into two major groups. The Parker faithful continued developing the bop idiom, mostly on the East coast, and were called "hard bop" musicians. Musicians such as Clifford Brown, Hank Mobley, Sonny Rollins, Art Blakey and Horace Silver were in this group. The Young followers were mostly on the West Coast and comprised musicians like Lennie Tristano, Gerry Mulligan, John Lewis and Miles Davis.

The musical distance between these two groups was

even greater than the geographical distance. While the hard bop people brought greater technical perfection and harmonic knowledge to their music, those involved with the cool movement moved jazz into a new classicist direction. In part, this classicist direction was a modern reworking of styles from the thirties and largely contained in material of the Count Basie band of that era. In part, it was an infusion of academic European music into jazz.

Whatever the roots of this new music, it was a reflection of the times. As Joachim Berendt comments, whereas "bebop captured the nervous restlessness of the forties... cool jazz reflected the resignation of men who live well, yet know that H-bombs are being stockpiled." It was the ultimate musical expression of the new atomic age, the cold war which was quietly being fought through subtle treachery on an international scale. It was a subtle music.

The greatest practitioner of this subtle and cool new jazz was Miles Davis. He was the master of musical understatement who examined more than anyone else the psychological effects of living in this post-war period. Leonard Feather states that he "reduced the searing flame of Gillespie to a low-glowing introverted matter." In many respects, he had to do this, for he couldn't compete on a technical scale with people like Gillespie and Parker. Although never the technical master of his instrument, Davis knew and utilized his limits beautifully. More his own man than almost anyone in the history of music, he copied no one while developing a style centering on the middle register of his trumpet where he was the strongest.

And he worked tirelessly to shape his phrases, to create a certain mood. Whereas Parker was more intent on spontaneous destruction, Davis was more concerned with meticulously engineering construction. His tone was one of great purity, full of softness and almost without vibrato or attack.

His first big musical break came in 1944 when he had a chance to play in the famous Billy Eckstine orchestra which included Charlie Parker, Dizzy Gillespie and Dexter Gordon. At that time his musical idol was Parker and he made most of Parker's New York gigs while attending the Juilliard School of Music. Eventually, Parker asked him to join him, and albums such as *Bird—The Savoy Recordings* and *Charlie Parker On Dial* from this association show the developing Davis style.

Leaving Parker in 1948, he worked and studied with a man who was to become one of modern jazz's greatest arrangers and composers, Gil Evans. The Davis-Evans association would produce the definitive statement of cool jazz in 1949 on the album *Birth Of The Cool* on the old Capitol label. Later, the association would turn out other masterpieces of modern jazz such as *Miles Ahead* and *Sketches of Spain*.

The early 1950s were a tough time for Davis, though, and the fame that the so-called Capitol recordings should have brought him never came. In some ways he found himself isolated in a strange no-man's-land of jazz. He had an intimate knowledge of the bebop style but he wasn't a convert to it. He was well acquainted with the music of Lester Young but he wasn't interested in simply perpetuating the Young sound. He was alone in that twilight space between major art forms where prophetic artists often find themselves, and he spent much time in the early fifties attempting to make this no-man's-land his own country.

During this search for a musical footing, he would produce some of the finest work of his career on albums such as *Miles Davis, Volumes 1 & 2, Blue 'n' Boogie, Tallest Trees* and *Bag's Groove*. The sparse sound with little technical dexterity began to emerge as a new, unique sound in jazz rather than as a mask for limitations. In exploring the loneliness he felt in that no-man's-land, he expressed much of the loneliness post-war modern man felt.

Success finally came for Davis in the mid-fifties, and he found himself the overwhelming hit of the Newport Jazz Festival. It was at this time that Coltrane came to work with Davis. The two musicians were alike in as many ways as they were different.

Coltrane was working with the organist Jimmy Smith when the call from Miles Davis came. After working the Philadelphia club scene with lesser-known musicians such as Shirley Scott and conga player Bill Carney, and continuing in a general depressed state about his music, he was playing a two-week engagement with Smith at a club called Spider Kelly's and feeling extremely excited about it. The two musicians worked very well together and Smith asked Coltrane to join him on a permanent basis.

He was seriously considering Smith's offer when drummer Philly Joe Jones called and told him that Miles Davis was forming a new group and wanted Coltrane to join it. After briefly discussing the matter with Naima, he accepted the Davis offer and joined them on their very first date together in Baltimore. The temperaments of the musicians fused beautifully on that opening night. A few days later, John and Naima were married. The pendulum was beginning to swing the other way for Coltrane.

The combination was unique. Davis, the rising avant-garde star of the cool movement, a type of musical James Dean, matched with one of the heavies of the hard bop school. A more blatant juxtaposition of style and technique is hard to imagine.

Yet underneath the outward appearances there was a strong philosophical similarity between the two musicians. Both were artistic rebels who were unable or unwilling to fit into the current state of the art and both had paid heavy dues for their positions in the jazz world. Coltrane was still a junkie, while Davis had kicked the habit in 1954. Both were lonely in many ways, because not many other musicians really understood what they were attempting to say. Both felt they had something unique and important to say and both were intensely searching for the proper way to say it.

The result was the creation of a rarefied creative atmosphere where growth and expression were constantly encouraged more than anything else. Nothing was really planned too much in advance and there was no rigid format for the group. As Simpkins relates, "It functioned instead through the medium of each other's feelings." There were few rehearsals and most of the education was immediately used on the bandstand.

It was the first time Coltrane was able to combine those two perennial extremes in his life, education and application of education, and place them under one roof. For Coltrane, it must have been like reflecting in public on ideas from all the interesting people, books and philosophies he had been exposed to in his life. No longer did the pendulum have to swing so far in the direction of one of the extremes. The bandstand itself was now a classroom.

In this environment Coltrane, for the first time, could begin the serious development of a distinct style. Those early apprenticeship years in the well-known bands had certainly been beneficial, but the benefits were almost all in the area of technique. The musicians he played with had been around for a few years and had time to develop their own styles and to develop audiences which expected these styles. There wasn't room enough in these bands for a person like Coltrane who was constantly growing and expanding his musical horizons.

The Coltrane style, though, was a tentative one during these early years with Davis. As Martin Williams notes in *The Jazz Tradition*, "He seemed more interested in discovery than in making finished statements, as though for the time being he was occupied with turning up a vocabulary with which future sentences, paragraphs, and essays might be built." This is evident on albums such as *'Round About Midnight, Steamin'* and *Workin'*. Here and there, one can detect a hesitancy and unwillingness to further define or pursue the musical images which dart in front of him like a wild herd of animals. Like some mad watercolor painter, he is only concerned with catching the scene in sweeping brush strokes and then ripping this sketch off the pad and starting a new one. Concentrating on the individual painting, pursuing one idea alone, he would miss the rest of the ideas rushing by at supersonic speed.

When ideas are pursued they usually lead into the thick undergrowth of an unexplored territory and come to a halt in an unsure fumble of notes, an incoherent babbling. Some type of barrier is reached which seems impossible to surmount given his present musical vocabulary. Various combinations of notes are quickly tried but ultimately he arrives at some musical dead end. The effect is often like the increasingly hectic motions of some small animal trying to escape from some great subterranean network of tunnels and passageways.

In the exotic musical kingdom he was beginning to create and explore, these stalemated positions he found himself in were less important than the speed and intensity with which he arrived; the trip was more important than the destination. Never in the history of jazz had anyone run the scales on a saxophone at the unbelievable speed that Coltrane was running them. It was almost supernatural at times and led some critics to speculate that he was attempting to further subdivide jazz rhythm from the popular eighth notes of bop into a new jazz idiom based on sixteenth notes.

The dense musical textures he was creating during this time with Miles Davis came to be termed his "sheets of sound" period. Jazz critic Ira Gitler coined the term and writes, "His multi-note improvisations were so thick and complex they were almost flowing out of the horn by themselves. That really hit me, the continuous flow of ideas without stopping. It was almost superhuman, and the amount of energy he was using could have powered a spaceship."

Not all critics, though, were in agreement with the assessment of Gitler. Many felt that his sound was harsh and freakish and lacked individuality. Reviewing his first album with Miles Davis, *The New Miles Davis Quintet*, Nat Hentoff commented how Coltrane's sound was a combination of Dexter Gordon, Sonny Rollins and Sonny Stitt. "But so far," he concluded, "there's very little Coltrane." On other albums such as *Tenor Madness*, *Paul Chambers* and *John Coltrane With Hank Mobley*, he also received mediocre reviews.

It was 1956 and he was appearing as a sideman on a number of albums apart from the dates with Miles Davis. There was his work with Tadd Dameron on *Mating Call*, with Sonny Rollins on *Tenor Madness*, and with Paul Chambers, Hank Mobley and Zoot Sims on *Tenor Conclave*. Yet despite his growing popularity with musicians, he was receiving very little recognition from those who held the power in the jazz world. At least he felt this to be the case and as a result became very discouraged with his music.

The Davis band was having its own problems too. Work dates were sporadic and the band members were lackadaisical, which caused the band to often be late or completely miss their engagements. Davis and Coltrane were also having personal problems. As Coltrane once said about Davis, "He's completely unpredictable. Sometimes he would walk off the stage after just playing a few notes, not even completing one chorus. If I asked him something about his music, I never knew how he was going to take it."

Coltrane's discouragement probably reached a low around the middle of 1956 when he and Naima moved to New York City for a short period. He was living in cheap hotel rooms—places like the Marie Antoinette where they had only one room, with the bathroom down the hall. He was picking up various dates by hanging around the musician's union. For awhile, he had been able to stop using drugs, but now, in New York, a friend in one of these hotels started him using them again. The old nemesis was back in full force. At the end of his musical rope, he wanted to quit music altogether and walked into the New York Post Office and filled out an application to be a postman.

In November of 1956 he abruptly left Miles Davis and returned to Philadelphia where he and Naima lived in his mother's house and where he worked less and less as he used more alcohol and drugs. He had been to this extreme a few times before and it was beginning to rule his life. However, this time he must have sensed that some final decision had to be made if he was going to reach his full potential as a musician: he would have to decide once and for all if he was going to live the rest of his life as a drug addict or as a musician. The two were not compatible in someone with such incredible potential as Coltrane. There

had to be a final decision in order for him to ever seriously pursue the limits of this potential.

• • •

Coltrane made the decision in the early spring of 1957.
He awoke one morning and told Naima and his mother
that he wanted to stop using drugs and asked for their
help. Realizing the problems that drugs had caused him
and his career, they were both overjoyed at the prospect
that he now wanted to quit and pledged to help in any way
they could.

He then retreated into his room, where he would battle
the terrible pains of withdrawal for the next few days. He
would live solely on water and leave the room only to go
to the bathroom. During the days he spent most of his time
praying and asking for God's help to see him through this
ordeal. When he spoke with Naima his thoughts were jumbled. Clearly, some incredible event was taking place in
that room.

One morning, about four days later, he walked out of
his room and announced to the family that he was no
longer addicted to heroin or alcohol. There was a certain
look of tranquillity on his face, a certain awestruck expression. He was extremely quiet.

Naima, concerned about his silence, asked him if something was wrong. He looked at her and told her that he had
a dream in which he heard this droning sound. "It was so
beautiful," he told her. She asked him to describe it and he

tried but found it impossible. He then went over to the piano and attempted to play it. But after a few minutes he gave up.

With this event, the search for the mysterious sound began. It was a search that would continue throughout his life and would cause him to create some of his most intense and emotional music. It became his own Holy Grail and the pursuit of it would lead him to the music of India, the Mideast and Africa and to a hypnotic chanting rhythm most easily discernible in compositions such as "India" from the 1961 *Impressions* and "Africa" from *Africa/Brass* the same year. In these and a number of other pieces from the early and mid-sixties, the bass repeated the same notes throughout the compositions, and this chant-like repetition served as a foundation for cosmic solo horn trajectories, often soaring to the very edge of his own musical universe.

The transformation resulting from his exorcism of drugs is best documented on the 1964 album *A Love Supreme*, recorded seven years after the events in 1957. Many view it as the finest work of his career. Coltrane's liner note comments are informative. "During the year 1957," he writes, "I experienced, by the grace of God, a spiritual awakening which was to lead me to a richer, fuller, more productive life. At that time, in gratitude, I humbly asked to be given the means and privilege to make others happy through music. I feel this has been granted through His grace." He describes a period of "irresolution" which prevailed and how he entered a phase which was "contradictory to the pledge and away from the esteemed path."

It's as if he is describing all of those drug-filled years from the late forties to the spring of 1957, the back-and-forth swings of his musical pendulum during his years with Gillespie, Bostic, Hodges and Davis—the powerful conflicts which pulled him in a number of directions, holding back something deep inside that desperately wanted to be set free.

Revealingly, *A Love Supreme* is divided into four major sections, the titles of which indicate the various stages in the spiritual life of an individual. The first part is entitled "Acknowledgment," the second part "Resolution," the third "Pursuance" and the fourth simply "Psalm." Many critics believe that these four words describe the progress of Coltrane's music after his "spiritual awakening" of 1957. By 1964, when *A Love Supreme* was recorded, a good argument could be made that his music had reached the final stage of this development and that most everything he played until the end of his life was a "psalm" or a prayer to God. Much of the music certainly bears out this conjecture.

In the spring of 1957, though, he was beginning this spiritual journey. It was a period of "acknowledgment" for him—acknowledgment of the great forces and powers of God and acknowledgment of the infinite possibilities open to the person who truly believes in these powers.

Overlapping this first stage and leading directly into the second stage of "resolution" was probably the most important event in his career, the last true apprenticeship in his life. It was a chance to learn and play with the underground high priest of the bop movement—Thelonious

Sphere Monk. More than anyone else, Monk would give Coltrane the space to work out and "acknowledge" the emotions he was feeling during this time, and the space to make certain "resolutions" about his life and his music. Monk would provide Coltrane the key to unlock all sorts of musical doors and free the dark and the beautiful visions Coltrane had seen throughout his life.

On the album cover a bearded man wearing a black beret stares worriedly as he plays a dusty old upright piano. On top of the piano sit a hand grenade, a revolver, binoculars, a burning candle and some wine bottles. A submachine gun is strapped over the man's right shoulder and next to his right foot is a detonator wired to a number of sticks of dynamite. Behind him, a Nazi storm trooper in full uniform is tied to a chair. A few feet to the left of the storm trooper a large cow stands looking out at us with his head slightly cocked to one side. Behind the cow a lovely young woman sits on a bale of hay wearing a khaki uniform, a red scarf and a beret. In her right hand she holds a submachine gun.

The album is *Underground Thelonious Monk*, produced by the great jazz producer Teo Macero. "A word about the cover photograph," writes Gil McKean in the album's liner notes. "Although the illustration on the album cover may seem a trifle bizarre to the uninitiated, knowing intimates of Monk will recognize the setting as that of his studio, an important part of his Manhattan apartment."

But the real Monk was even more bizarre than the album cover suggests. For one thing, Monk did not have an upright piano but rather a grand piano and it was situated in the kitchen of his apartment rather than the living room. On top of the grand piano are forgotten souvenirs, phone books, a typewriter, old magazines and groceries.

The real Monk is one of the unique figures in the history of jazz. Born in 1920, he grew up in New York and was first influenced by Duke Ellington, Fats Waller and the great stride pianist James P. Johnson. At the age of eleven he began weekly piano lessons at 75 cents an hour, and by fourteen he was playing jazz at hard-time Harlem "rent parties." He soon began turning up every Wednesday for amateur night at the Apollo Theater. He won so often that he was eventually barred from the show. As the February 1964 *Time* magazine noted, "He was playing stride piano— a single note on the first and third beats of the bar, a chord on the second and fourth. Unable to play with the wizardry of Art Tatum or Teddy Wilson, though, he found a way of his own. His small hands and his unusual harmonic sense made his style unique."

When he was sixteen years old he decided that he had enough education, or at least as much as he could take, and quit high school to go on tour with a faith healer. But within a year he was back in New York, playing the piano at Kelly's Stable on 52nd Street. *Time* notes that, "The street was jumping in those days, and in advance of the vogue, Monk bought a zoot suit and grew a beard."

It was the mid-forties and the jazz world was dominated by the crushing music of swing. Charlie Parker and Dizzy Gillespie were beginning to meet regularly at Minton's to explore the developing new music of bebop.

Monk held the piano chair during these famous musical engagements at Minton's. Perhaps more than anyone else, Monk was the needling inspiration to the others. The boldness of his harmonies forced the horn players into flights the likes of which had never been heard. Eventually, he became the "High Priest of Bebop."

But life is not always easy at the top, especially for one who doesn't really want to be there, who is basically a recluse, who perpetually pushes his creativity to the tip of the art form's avant-garde fringe area. It is always lonely there because most have burnt out at this stage of their creativity. Monk never did, but he must have felt like a survivor at Valley Forge surveying the fallen around him. The fallen were fellow musicians who had lost themselves in narcotic fogs, died early in squalor and disgrace or abandoned their promise, to fall silent on their instruments.

It was lonely for Monk because when bop drifted out of Harlem and into wider popularity after the war, Monk found himself outside the mainstream of jazz. His playing was a lean, dissonant, unresolved jazz that most players found extremely difficult to accompany. Many musicians resented him and he quickly lost a number of steady jobs. During this time he spent a lot of time in his room staring at the picture of Billie Holiday tacked to his ceiling. He also composed some of his famous pieces such as "Round Midnight," "Well, You Needn't" and "Ruby, My Dear."

In 1951 Monk's situation reached a low point when he was arrested with pianist Bud Powell for possession of heroin. Monk had been "clean" but refused to let Powell take the rap alone and, as a result, spent sixty days in jail. When he was released the police canceled his important cabaret card, a document required of all entertainers who appear in New York nightclubs. Losing the card cost Monk his slender livelihood.

During these bleak years he was sustained by an amazing woman. Her official name was the Baroness Pannonica de Koenigswarter. She was the daughter of the British banker Nathaniel Charles Rothschild and the sister of the 3rd Baron Rothschild. The baroness, though, had abandoned her world of long, historical names to become a hard-core New York night person in search of the avantgarde. Discovering the uniquely original music of Monk made her a close friend, mascot and champion of the new style he was juxtaposing against a predominantly cool period in jazz.

The Baroness, or "Nica" as she came to be known, followed Monk all over town. She gave him rides, rooms to compose and play in and, in 1957, help in getting back the vital cabaret card. One night, soon after regaining his cabaret card, Monk spent the evening in the Baroness' apartment listening to another musician, also down on his luck, named John Coltrane. During the evening Coltrane played "Monk's Mood," an original Monk composition. Monk liked his treatment of it so well that he asked Coltrane to join his group. Their engagement was at a place called the Five Spot in New York's East Village.

The engagement at the Five Spot, beginning in the spring of 1957 and carrying on well into the following fall, became one of the most important dates in the history of jazz. The Thelonious Monk Quartet, with Ahmed Abdul-Malik on bass, Roy Haynes on drums, Monk on piano and Coltrane on saxophone, was captured live at the Five Spot in April 1957 on the old Jazzland record label. The album is now known as *Discovery* and it is an important part of the Coltrane discography.

Nat Hentoff compares it to Louis Armstrong playing second cornet to King Oliver at the Royal Garden Cafe in Chicago in the 1920s. It was at the Five Spot that Hentoff, probably the most adamant attacker of Coltrane's music through his reviews in *Down Beat*, was finally transformed into a Coltrane convert. As he remembers, "I was there nearly every night all the weeks Monk and Trane played the Five Spot, and it was there I finally understood how nonpareil a musician, how dauntless an explorer Coltrane was. The excitement was so heady that soon musicians were standing two and three deep at the bar of the Five Spot nearly every night." Another Coltrane critic, Bill Cole, compares it to the work of Gillespie and Parker during the forties.

Probably more than anything else, Monk taught Coltrane about the use of musical space, those important silent intervals between the notes and chords. Monk's music contained vast amounts of space, and for the musicians playing with him it was often a two-edged sword: the space could be molded and shaped like the space theorized in Einstein's calculations and new musical dimensions could be approximated, or the space could engulf the musician. As Coltrane once remarked about Monk's music,

"If you didn't keep aware all the time of what was going on, you'd suddenly feel as if you'd stepped into a hole without a bottom to it." McCoy Tyner adds that Monk taught Coltrane "when to lay out and let somebody else fill the space, or just leave the space open." For Coltrane, who had recently been experimenting with lightning-fast delivery during his sheets of sound period with Davis, it was a strong juxtaposition and an important lesson.

Unlike almost all the other famous musicians Coltrane had played with, Monk's accompaniment was not an ongoing, systematic spacing of chords but rather the placing of sounds in just the right spots at the right times. It was somewhat like dancing through a musical minefield with charges going off every few seconds: one never could anticipate exactly where and when the next charge would detonate but after it happened it seemed to make brilliant musical sense.

Then, too, there was the space created by Monk's absence from the bandstand. Often, after his solo Monk would rise from the piano, bending and whirling, pivoting around while stomping his feet and waving his hands. The effect was like watching a huge windup doll. Iggy Termini, one of the owners of the Five Spot, was present at the club during this time and recalls that Monk would sometimes wander into the kitchen after his strange little dance and "start talking with the dishwasher about God knows what. Once in a while he'd fall asleep at the piano, and when it was time for him to come in again, he'd wake up and start playing, just like that."

Left with Roy Haynes and Ahmed Abdul-Malik on the bandstand, Coltrane struggled to fend for himself, searching out the landscape carefully among the small, silent, intervals that were so much a part of the music, precariously dancing through the Monkian minefield, avoiding getting blown back by all the explosions, trying not to fall into bottomless musical holes. As Hentoff remarks in *Jazz Is*, Monk creates a "total musical microcosm, and for musicians who play with him the challenge is to keep your balance, to stay with Monk, no matter where his unpredictably intricate imagination leads—and at the same time, play yourself, be yourself." It was a monumental challenge for Coltrane.

But Coltrane met the challenge and came to view Monk as a modern replacement for his father and grandfather who had died at such an early age in his life. To Coltrane, Monk was the greatest teacher he had ever encountered. His respect for Monk is evidenced in an interview from the September 1960, issue of *Down Beat* with critic Don DeMichael. In the interview Coltrane says, "Working with Monk brought me close to a musical architect of the highest order. I felt I learned from him in every way—through the senses, theoretically, technically. I would talk to Monk about musical problems, and he would sit at the piano and show me the answers just by playing them. I could watch him play and find out things I wanted to know. Also, I could see a lot of things I didn't know about at all."

There were still a lot of things Coltrane didn't know about. One was a method called false fingering, or "multiphonics," whereby two or three notes were played at one time on tenor. As Coltrane relates, "It's done by false fingering and adjusting your lips, and if it's done right you get triads." Another thing Coltrane learned with Monk was the technique of playing long solos on pieces to find new conceptions for the solo. He remarks that "It got so I would go as far as possible on one phrase until I ran out of ideas." Harmonic structure begin to be fully explored with Monk. "The harmonies got to be an obsession for me," Coltrane notes. "Sometimes I'd think I was making music through the wrong end of a magnifying glass."

And during this period with Monk there are indications he was further developing some of the earlier ideas which Dennis Sandole had exposed him to at the Ornstein School of Music in Philadelphia. His wife Naima would often come to the Five Spot with a tape recorder and transcribe as many complete sets as possible. Then, later that night, they would listen to the evening's tape for criticism and study.

One evening while listening to the tapes, Coltrane heard some strange sounds he had never heard before on the Monk ballad "Ruby, My Dear." Naima had gone to sleep but he woke her up and asked for her assistance in identifying the source of the mysterious sound he was hearing. She knew classical music better than he did and after listening for a while said it sounded like Ravel's "Daphnis and Chloe" and that the unique sound he was getting from his tenor was like a harp.

This began many intensive months of studying the

harp. To Coltrane, the gorgeous, shimmering sounds which could be obtained from it were almost sacred. While studying the harp he listened mostly to an advanced European harpist named Salzeda and particularly Salzeda's "Transcriptions For Two Harps." For a period of a few months he listened constantly to this recording and often went to sleep at night by it. The fruit of his efforts to understand the harp would later be demonstrated in some of the late albums of his career and would be a major factor in the spiritual sound these albums accomplished.

Toward the end of 1957, Monk became tired of working and disbanded the group. Coltrane was on his own again, a lot wiser and stronger than before.

Emergence

*A*part from his work with Monk and the transformation he experienced by giving up drugs, 1957 was an important year for Coltrane in other respects. For one thing it was his most prolific recording year to date.

During 1957 he can be heard on over twenty albums, and significantly there is a wide range of styles and techniques in these works. If he had yet to receive wide recognition in the jazz world and critical acclaim, Coltrane was becoming well-known and respected by his fellow musicians. A few of these dates deserve mention.

There was his work with fellow tenorist Johnny Griffin on *Johnny Griffin—A Blowing Session*; with pianist Mal Waldron on *Mal Waldron Sextet*; with Paul Quinichette on *John Coltrane-Paul Quinichette Quintet*; with Red Garland on a number of late 1957 recordings such as *High Pressure, Dig It* and *Soul Junction*; with Tadd Dameron on *Coltrane Plays For Lovers*; and with Art Blakey on *Art Blakey Big Band*. Besides this distinguished group of jazz luminaries, he would also work and record with people like Kenny Burrell, Jackie McLean, Hank Mobley, Paul Chambers, Oscar Pettiford, Donald Byrd and Gigi Gryce.

But his most important work from this period is contained on the albums which represent his first work as a leader rather than as a sideman, for it was during 1957 that he first began making records under his own name. His first album as a leader, entitled *The First Trane*, is available today under the reissue title *More Lasting Than Bronze*. Two albums from the latter part of 1957, *Traneing In* and *Wheelin' And Dealin'*, show Coltrane beginning to flex some of his developing musical muscle with some straight ahead extended solos.

And there is also *Blue Trane*, which may represent the most important work from this period because of the many facets of his developing style revealed. In "I'm Old Fashioned" he experiments with a device which would later play an extremely important part in his music. As C.O. Simpkins remarks, "he plays with shifting accents, alternating delicately, his sound with that of the piano," therefore creating a "feeling of floating slowly upward." Later in his career, in the mid-sixties, he would again employ this device in some of his high-energy pieces to push the band to new levels.

The title tune from *Blue Trane* was the subject of an article by critic Zita Carno in the October and November 1959 issue of *Jazz Review* magazine. Carno, a classical pianist and graduate of the Manhattan School of Music, became the foremost Coltrane supporter during this period, and her article in *Jazz Review* remains one of the finest technical pieces ever written about Coltrane. In part she notes that "Blue Trane" has a "powerful blues line" and is "brooding and mysterious like a chant, with more than just the meaning of the blues in it." She discusses the constant "building up" of high energy on his solo and his tendency to stay in the high register of his horn.

Elsewhere in the article Carno makes some interesting general observations about the Coltrane style. "His range," she notes, "is something to marvel at: a full three octaves upward from the lowest note obtainable on the horn." But she finds the thing that makes the Coltrane style unique is not the range but rather the "equality of strength in all registers." His sound is "just as clear, full and unforced in the topmost notes as it is down at the bottom." Commenting on the extremely rapid technique he was developing during this period, which Ira Gitler termed sheets of sound, Carno remarks that it consists of "very long phrases played at such an extremely rapid tempo that the notes he plays cease to be mere notes and fuse into a continuous flow of pure sound."

There were other indications in 1957 that he was finally emerging from the dark, subterranean depths of the jazz underground which he had lived in for all those years. Bob Weinstock, the founder of Prestige Records, learned of Coltrane's work during the Coltrane-Davis association and, prompted by Red Garland, decided to sign Coltrane to a two-year recording contract. For the first time in his career, it was now possible for a wider group of people to hear Coltrane's music.

And, through reassessments of his music by influential critics such as Nat Hentoff, it was possible that a wider group of people might be able to read about his music. Hentoff was an important jazz critic for the large, general circulation publication of the jazz world, *Down Beat* magazine. Probably more than anything else at the time, exposure in *Down Beat* could make, or break, a jazz artist. More a promotional tool for the jazz establishment than a showcase for the avant-garde in these years, Coltrane's hard sound usually received little attention in *Down Beat*. His harsh, strident, hot sound went perhaps too much against the grain in the predominantly "cool" period of jazz.

By the end of 1957, though, there was a shift in the attitude of *Down Beat* toward Coltrane and he began receiving good reviews of his music in the magazine. One of the first enthusiastic reviews in the magazine was by Dom Ceruli in the December 26, 1957, issue. Ceruli wrote that "his playing is constantly tense and searching" and "always a thrilling experience." Enthusiastic reviews by other critics such as Hentoff would soon follow. And in the magazine's annual Reader's Poll of popular musicians, Coltrane placed 11th in the regular saxophone category. Stan Getz placed first and Sonny Rollins placed second.

After leaving Monk, Coltrane had thoughts of permanently going on his own. Many people at the Five Spot had encouraged him to do so and he had much support from fellow musicians in this direction. He was seriously considering setting off on his own when Miles Davis called him one day. Davis had wanted Coltrane to return for some time now, especially after hearing him with Monk at the Five Spot. All Davis said to Coltrane when he called was "I want you back" and Coltrane replied, with equal simplicity, "All right."

The second association with Miles Davis, starting in December of 1957, would last a little more than two years and would conclude his final years as an apprentice to other famous leaders. As it was with the year 1957, these two years would also be very musically prolific for Coltrane and he would appear on approximately twenty-five records either in a quasi-leadership role or as a front line sideman.

There would be his important work with the famous French composer Michael Legrand on *Legrand Jazz*, which exposed him to the most intricate voicing and textures he had ever encountered in popular music. The Legrand songs were complex, with unusual harmonic structures. There would be his work with the legendary fluegelhornist Wilbur Harden on important works such as *Bahia, Jazz Way Out, Tanganyika Strut,* and the famous Stardust sessions. There would be his work with vibraphonist Milt Jackson on *Bags And Trane,* with Cannonball Adderley on *Cannonball Adderley Quintet In Chicago,* and with bassist Paul Chambers and drummer Jimmy Cobb, both of whom appeared on most of the records during this time.

His first association with Davis in 1955 and 1956 was an experimental period where various musical ideas were tested, possible vocabularies explored, and a tentative style suggested. The Miles Davis band of the mid-fifties was a jazz laboratory where new musical ideas were blended and new forms created. Coltrane, though, discovered no "secret formula" in this laboratory. The time was not yet right. He was still testing, seeing how far he might be able to go some day with his instrument. He was still on drugs and often strung out, and did not have the inner strength to embark on a serious pursuit of the possibilities in jazz music.

But now, in December of 1957, things were different. He had, for the first time in his life, the inner strength and discipline to embark on a great musical odyssey. There had been a painful withdrawal from drugs and an accompanying spiritual rebirth, and he was now a man with a clear vision, a powerful revelation to attempt to communicate to others. His recent exposure to the great Monk had given him thoughts about the creation of a new architecture of jazz and, at the same time, a certain discipline and strength to construct this new architecture.

And Davis had changed, too. As Coltrane relates in the September 29, 1960, issue of *Down Beat* magazine "I found Miles in the midst of another stage of his musical development. There was one time in his past that he devoted to multichorded structures. He was interested in chords for their own sake. But now it seemed that he was moving in the opposite direction, to the use of fewer and fewer chord changes. He used tunes with free-flowing lines and chordal direction. This approach allowed the soloist the choice of playing chordally (vertically) or melodically (horizontally)."

Coltrane was the soloist who made the greatest use of Davis' free-flowing lines. In this new musical environment he found it easier to apply the harmonic ideas he had at the time. He could "stack" chords. As he relates in *Down Beat*, "On a C7, I sometimes superimposed an Eb7, up to an F#7, down to an F. That way I could play three chords on one.

But on the other hand, if I wanted to, I could play melodically. Miles' music gave me plenty of freedom."

During this time he was further developing his sheets of sound technique. It was an attempt at creating a great sweeping harp-like sound at which members of the French impressionistic school, such as Ravel, were so adept. In many ways, Coltrane, enchanted by the capabilities of the harp, was attempting to make the saxophone into a type of harp.

The notes came dancing out of his horn at superhuman speed during these years and to many they may have appeared as sheets of sound. But in slow motion one can see that the sheets are made from a continuous application of his technique of stacking chords and playing three chords on one. As Coltrane relates in *Down Beat*, "I was beginning to apply the three-on-one chord approach, and at the time the tendency was to play the entire scale of each chord. Therefore, they were usually played fast and sometimes sounded like glisses."

Throughout the music of this period, Coltrane placed strange and unusual accents on various notes. As he once commented to Davis, he was increasingly committed to "getting it all in." Many times this fast, free-flowing process of creation involved fitting square pegs into round holes. As Coltrane remarks "I found there were a certain number of chord progressions to play in a given time and sometimes what I played didn't work out in eighth notes, sixteenth notes, or triplets." Therefore, he "had to put the notes in uneven groups like fives and sevens in order to get them all in."

His approach was so sweepingly vast and uniquely · bold that he no longer thought in terms of musical notes but rather in terms of groups of notes. "I tried," he recalls in *Down Beat*, "to place these groups on the accents and emphasize the strong beats—maybe on two here and on four over at the end." Sometimes it worked but other times it clashed harmonically with the piano.

The juxtaposition of musical styles almost in direct counterpoint to each other would again create some important music. As it had been with their first association, the sophisticated simplicity of Davis would provide the perfect environment for Coltrane's increasingly complex solos and offer a fascinating study of the creative process at work in two major artists running close to full throttle.

In Davis' attempt to play with great simplicity, his improvisations were slowly freed from the underlying structure of chord changes and gradually came to be based on scales. An example of this technique can be heard in the Gil Evans arrangement of "I Love You, Porgy" from Gershwin's famous work *Porgy And Bess*. As Davis relates, "When Gil wrote the arrangement...he only wrote a scale for me to play. No chords." This gave Davis "a lot more freedom and space to hear things." In this important new method of jazz improvisation, the chords were no longer defined by the constantly changing harmonies of a harmonic structure and every chord that corresponded to a "mode," or scale, was allowed.

The Coltrane-Davis combination recorded five albums

employing the Davis experiments in modal improvisation with varying degrees of intensity and success. There were *Jazz Track* and *Miles And Monk At Newport* from 1958, and *Someday My Prince Will Come* from 1961. And, in a class by themselves, were two other albums—1958's *Milestones* and 1959's *Kind Of Blue*. These two would become some of the most important music in jazz history.

• • •

The time was the late fifties and America and the world were in a state of transition. President Eisenhower was sending army paratroopers to Central High School in Little Rock, Arkansas, to guarantee the safe enrollment of nine black students at the recently desegregated school. The Russians had launched a small silver ball called Sputnik into orbit around the earth. A lawyer from Havana named Fidel Castro had established a dictatorship in Cuba.

And jazz was in another state of transition. The "cool" jazz reaction to the complexities of the Parkeresque bebop and the return to a more simplistic approach had now itself evolved into a complex music. Cool jazz was acquiring many institutional characteristics and in the process the music was becoming bogged down in the dense musical swamp it had created.

Emerging musicians such as John Lewis of the Modern Jazz Quartet and Dave Brubeck of the Dave Brubeck Quartet brought new, complex European classical styles into jazz. Classically trained and influenced by modern

European composers such as Darius Milhaud, Brubeck imported many classical devices into jazz, such as atonality, fugue and counterpoint. Lewis, the former anthropology student and founder of the famous Modern Jazz Quartet, was also a strong classicist who possessed a vast knowledge of European musical forms.

One has only to listen to introverted, complex and structured works as Brubeck's *Time Out* album or Lewis compositions such as "Vendome," "Concorde," "Milano" and "Sun Dance" to realize that this form of jazz was working itself into a type of dilemma, a musical straitjacket of sorts. Experiments in unusual time signatures such as "Blue Rondo A La Turk" in 9/8 and "Take Five" in 5/4 from *Time Out* left little space for improvisation. In many ways this new jazz, sometimes called "cool" and sometimes simply "modern," was a small chamber group hybrid of the Ellington and Basie swing music of the thirties and forties. Unlike the Ellington and Basie music, though, modern jazz left little room for spontaneous expression from musicians who played it. Only a few, like Milt Jackson, could improvise in the idiom. The others, surrounded by complex chords and harmonies, found freeform improvisation increasingly difficult as they became stuck in the intricate, intellectual textures of the music.

Musicians like Miles Davis and Oliver Nelson proposed possible escape routes from this musical quagmire. Nelson, an exceptionally gifted composer and musician, arrived on the New York jazz scene in 1959 and came to realize that the music must be given back to simpler forms in order for it to progress in the coming decade. In 1960, he wrote a tune called "Stolen Moments," and in 1961 he recorded an album, *The Blues And The Abstract Truth.* "Stolen Moments" was one of the six original Nelson compositions on the album. Along with Davis' *Kind Of Blue*, the Nelson work hypothesized a realistic way out of the stalemate and over the years has come to be regarded by many critics as one of the ten most important jazz albums in history. The honor is well-deserved.

During a period of intensive soul-searching to find his true musical self, the young Nelson wrote the six compositions in a free form which allowed musical ideas to determine the form and shape of the composition. As he states on the liner notes to *Blues And The Abstract Truth*, "The blues, which is a twelve-bar form, and the form and chord structure of 'I've Got Rhythm,' being 32 measures in length, was my material for all the compositions on this album. The augmentation of the forms themselves comes from thematic motifs and melodic ideas."

The experiment worked brilliantly and a composition like "Stolen Moments" only seems better with time, like a fine dusty old Bordeaux wine, so that it eventually comes to represent and symbolize a particular period in our history better than anything else. For the real importance of this album was finally not in the exclusive domain of the jazz world and some of the fairly esoteric struggles between various schools of jazz but rather in the much wider domain of history in general. More than offering an alternative to another form of jazz, a tune like "Stolen

Moments" offered expression of the general feeling of living in a particular period of time, not just for jazz musicians but for all Americans.

Coltrane was not on the album but, interestingly enough, many former and future Coltrane alumni were present. Eric Dolphy, Coltrane's closest friend and prodigy, was on alto saxophone and flute. Paul Chambers, his frequent session partner, was on bass. Roy Haynes, his future recording partner, was on drums, and Bill Evans was on piano. And finally, there was Oliver Nelson, who was influenced by both Coltrane and Rollins. Coltrane was not present on the date but the music echoed many of his and Miles Davis' concerns and ideas. These ideas were expressed brilliantly on the landmark *Milestones* and *Kind Of Blue*. It was from these that Nelson drew much of his inspiration for *Blues And The Abstract Truth*.

Milestones, recorded in April 1958, was the first album to emerge from the second Davis-Coltrane association. In addition to the original rhythm section of Red Garland on piano, Paul Chambers on bass and Philly Joe Jones on drums, Davis had added a new wizard of the alto sax with the addition of Cannonball Adderley. The voicing of Adderley, lighter and lower in the horn's register, provided a fascinating contrast to Coltrane's stratospheric tenor flights.

The album contained such complex tunes as Monk's "Straight, No Chaser" and Jackie McLean's "Dr. Jackle." In the new Davis band they served as stimulating departure points for Coltrane in his exploration of the new modal method of improvisation. *Milestone*'s title piece was written in G minor and made use of the key's Dorian and natural minor. As critic Bill Cole notes, "This gave Trane much more room to play rhythmic lines and thus his improvisation became longer." More and more the music was moving away from linear types of chordal progressions and toward tonal centers, away from the traditional linear method of expression and toward the nonlinear circular form. It had never been attempted in jazz, but it was a major feature of Indian music, and especially the Indian raga.

The rest of 1958 and the early part of 1959 would be an extremely busy time for Coltrane and he would be recorded on almost fifteen albums. Most of the time his role was that of front-line sideman. It was the time of the "blowing sessions" where bands would quickly materialize for recording dates, decide what they would play while in the studio, record some hard-driving horn work on standard material and then separate. Coltrane probably appeared on more of these blowing sessions than anyone else during this time and received a good amount of criticism from the jazz community for this prolific stretch of his career. Their major complaint was that it was now time for him to assume a leadership role and to stop spreading himself so thin by playing with all these different stylists. They had been telling him to do so since his engagement with Monk at the Five Spot and were now angry with him for not following their advice.

They were right in a sense. For after all those long hours of practice, often through the entire night, after the experience of playing with people such as Gillespie,

Hodges, Bostic, Vinson, Davis and Monk, after intense reading of all types of books, after a nightmarish existence in the twilight zone of drug addiction, after the many wonderful friendships he had established with people like Eric Dolphy, Thelonious Monk and Calvin Massey, after all these things and many more, he had developed a unique perspective on life and this perspective was increasingly difficult to express as a sideman.

However, by playing with all these different people Coltrane soaked up much information about his instrument and the possibilities within it. And too, the constant stimulus of recording dates made him a stronger and more disciplined musician. It was as if he was sharpening his musical armor before entering the center arena of the music.

So it is significant that the last album he would ever record as a sideman was *Kind Of Blue*. It was the album which would mark an end to a period in his life which had lasted more than ten years, a period of apprenticeship, a period of great personal growth, and of great spiritual insight. It was the final apprenticeship experience he would have to go through because when he left this historic recording date with Davis in April of 1959 he finally believed he had the necessary skills to communicate his unique musical perspective and vision to a growing audience increasingly anxious to hear his powerful emerging sound.

Kind Of Blue, recorded in March and April of 1959, featured the regular Miles Davis Sextet with the exceptions of Bill Evans, rather than Red Garland on piano, and Jimmy

Cobb, rather than Philly Joe Jones, on drums. It was the seminal Davis experiment in modality as a basis for improvisation, eloquently stating the thoughts of Davis on the subject and, with equal eloquence, letting the other musicians state their thoughts also. The album contains modal pieces with harmonic challenges cut to a minimum. This allows the soloist to invent on a single chord or scale for sixteen measures or as long as he likes.

Davis attempted to make the project as spontaneous as possible and conceived the ideas for the various tunes on the album only hours before the recording dates. He arrived in the studio with broad sketches of what he wanted to accomplish. The group had never played the pieces before and their interpretations of Davis' original sketches are as spontaneous as possible. On the album's liner notes, Bill Evans comments that "Although it is not uncommon for a jazz musician to be expected to improvise on new material at a recording session, the character of these pieces represents a particular challenge." Most of the improvisation was done using points of departure that jazzmen had only rarely undertaken.

For example, the tune "So What" asks the improviser to create his melody from one assigned Dorian mode for sixteen measures, then move a half-step up for eight measures and then move back to the first mode for a final eight measures. It presented a unique challenge but at the same time a unique opportunity to the musicians. The composition "All Blues" is a series of five scales, each to be played as long as the soloist wishes until he has completed the series.

"Blue In Green," a ten-measure composition following a four-measure introduction, allows the soloists to play in various augmentation and diminution of time values. "Flamenco Sketches," a haunting 6/8 twelve-measure blues, produces its mood through only a few modal changes. Finally, "Freddie Freeloader" is a twelve-measure blues form given a certain dynamic form by effective melodic and rhythmic simplicity.

A strong, sure, mature Coltrane is heard throughout the album. There is no longer the hesitancy in his playing which he had been attempting to shake free of through the fifties. And gone is much of the harsh, strident sound he was lambasted for by critics. Jazz critic Whitney Balliett aired some of these frequent criticisms about Coltrane's music in an article in *The New Yorker* from the fifties, remarking that "Coltrane's tone is harsh, flat, querulous, and at times vindictive" and that "His tone is bleaker than need be, many of his notes are useless, and his rhythmic methods are frequently just clothes flung all over a room." Flung over the rooms, one might add, the musical rooms he sometimes found himself trapped in after running down a number of passageways with his horn at supersonic speed; the inescapable positions he often arrived at during his first association with Davis, and the difficult places that Monk's lessons in advanced harmonics had put him into in the last few years.

In a sense, some of these critical observations are true. Coltrane, the perpetual extremist, had taken the harmonic element of music to an extreme while, at the same time, giving less and less attention to its melodic and rhythmic elements. Melody and rhythm were the "clothes" which, Balliett observed, Coltrane "flung" around the room.

The noted jazz critic Martin Williams offers an interesting speculation on this point in his book *The Jazz Tradition*. "From one point of view," he writes, "the post-Monk Coltrane had pushed jazz harmonies as far as they could go. From another, such complex, sophisticated knowledge set its own trap, and Coltrane, still a vertical thinker, careened around like a laboratory hamster trapped in a three-dimensional harmonic maze of his own making." He was trapped, as he repeatedly told Miles Davis, by trying to get "it all in."

With *Milestones* he saw a possible way out of his stalemated position, a hint of light far off in the distance at the end of the tunnel he was in. With *Kind Of Blue*, he approached this light and began to realize that he might be able to escape into truly unexplored territory, escape out into the open, brilliant midday light of a new musical world. The album opened all types of musical doors and suggested ways out of the strange musical funhouse he found himself in.

The emerging Coltrane sound is heard throughout *Kind Of Blue*, but it is on "So What" and "All Blues" that he is most prophetic about the possibilities which lay ahead, outside the tunnel. As Martin Williams observes, "He met the challenges of 'So What' and 'All Blues' like a man who saw, or thought he saw, an exit from the maze."

On "All Blues" Davis sets a soft, nostalgic, reflective

mood with his introductory solo. It is as if some old friends are getting together on a park bench to remember the past. In a real sense this is what happens. Coltrane's horn then enters and adds to the spirit of reflection. In some ways he seems to be answering the solo of Miles and musically discussing some of the things he had once learned but had forgotten or placed in some far corner of his mind. Things like the warm, melodic voicings of Johnny Hodges, who he had admired through the thirties and had played with in the forties. It was the ballad he had needed to do for a long time, the quiet, musical reflection about his neglected roots in the midst of all the blowing sessions. Davis and Coltrane, those intense musical explorers, had now reached a peaceful mountain lake one might find in the higher parts of Yosemite. Finally there could be some rest from the struggle. A new musical altitude is reached and the air is fresh, clear and invigorating.

The composition "So What" still provides the best musical lament to this period of history. After the initial statement of the simple two-note theme, Davis' trumpet explodes into a brilliant summation of ideas swirling about in his mind for years. Coltrane then enters playing some of the most spontaneous, inventive music he had ever played. The ideas are magnificent and it is apparent that Coltrane's time as a sideman is ending. They are majestic, elegant ideas and must have suggested the need for a new musical environment to develop them. He realized that he must soon become a leader.

Apart from the important and reflective statements

Kind of Blue made and the temporary peace it provided those two intense soldiers on the front line of jazz, it was also a prophetic work. In many ways it was a direct precursor to the group experiments in free jazz which were conducted during the sixties by Ornette Coleman on *Free Jazz* and by Coltrane himself on *Ascension*. And *Kind of Blue* set off a chain reaction in future Davis albums which led directly into much of the heart of the electronic jazz movement which surfaced in the sixties and the seventies—in the sixties in the legendary *In A Silent Way*, followed a few years later in the early seventies by an electronic elaboration of past Davis ideas on *Bitches Brew*. The Davis ideas, the chain reaction started by *Kind Of Blue*, led into the music of Josef Zawinul and Weather Report in the seventies.

Jazz of the late fifties. As Martin Williams notes, it was a time of "surface simplicity" and of "cutting back, opening up, and airing out the density of modern jazz," a time which "involved less emphasis on complex harmonic background and a greater emphasis on melody."

It was a period in jazz brought about and expressed largely through the music of Miles Davis and the increasingly powerful and original voice of John Coltrane.

Part Two
Prophet

Summit

After a life as sideman to more major jazz musicians than anyone else, Coltrane found it necessary to move on, to become a teacher himself and take others under his musical wing. In many ways it was a desire to share with others ideas musicians like Charlie Parker, Thelonious Monk, Miles Davis, Johnny Hodges and Dizzy Gillespie had given him. In many ways it was a need to communicate the feelings about his life up to then: his experiences with drugs, the early deaths of people very close to him, the exotic and esoteric teachings he had been exposed to for many years, the love he had for his family and the spiritual rebirth he went through in the late fifties.

It was that special moment when some move on from apprentices to teachers, from disciples to prophets. Musicians like Art Blakey, Horace Silver and Charles Mingus had realized this moment earlier and were now all firmly committed to teaching others some of the secrets which had been carefully handed to them by their own teachers under their own apprenticeships. Coltrane was soon to join this elite group of teachers. They were like a small band of explorers pushing into a new frontier.

Coltrane was thirty three years old at the time and finally decided to draw lines in his life and make a strong stand.

Encouraged by the incredible possibilities for improvisation which the modal theories of Miles Davis opened to him, he began doing something with more intensity and dedication than almost anything else he had ever done.

He began composing music.

The compositions were very personal in nature and centered on the people and places he loved: "Naima" for his wife; "Cousin Mary" for the cousin he had grown up with in North Carolina and lived with in Philadelphia (Mary really served as the surrogate sister for the real sister he never had); "Syeeda's Flute Song" for his ten-year-old stepdaughter; "Like Sonny" for his friend Sonny Rollins; and "Mr. P.C." for his favorite drummer Paul Chambers. They were also about places and concepts very close to him—the memory of Greenwich Village in the early fifties and the heroin fog he moved in found expression in "Village Blues," while "Fifth House" referred to his astrological sign.

This period followed April 1959's *Kind Of Blue* and lasted through December 1959. It brought many of Coltrane's earlier concepts, scattered through his own universe like vast cosmic clouds, together, calling them home like wandering ghosts. It was a time of creative implosion rather than an outward explosion. In the process he began to realize the sources of his power and to understand its gravitational nature.

The Coltrane family was living in a small house in the Queens section of New York. During this time, music completely possessed him and he would work intensely for periods of two to four weeks and then rest for a few weeks. He carried the saxophone everywhere he went during this time, as if it were some medium, a type of crystal ball, which could unexpectedly reveal certain things to him in fleeting moments of creativity. He wore it around his neck at the dinner table and would sit on the edge of his bed late into the night, thinking, with the horn strapped to his neck. Often he would fall asleep with it on, and Naima would have to remove it and put him to bed. Strewn about the house, sometimes in piles a few feet high, were hundreds of books on amazingly diverse subjects such as math, art, physics, biology, philosophy, psychology and religion. His friend Bill Evans had recommended Krishnamurti's *Commentaries on Living* and Sonny Rollins had recommended *Autobiography of a Yogi*. There were books by Edgar Cayce, Kahlil Gibran, Plato and Aristotle. There were books on Scientology and Egyptology.

The personal compositions were recorded on the two landmark albums *Giant Steps* and *Coltrane Jazz*. Both albums, and especially *Giant Steps*, mark his emergence as a major jazz composer. His saxophone has a new strength and sureness, and the tentativeness from his sheets of sound period with Davis is gone. It is less exploratory and more concerned with communicating the fruits of past explorations, rather than the ever-present current explorations. C.O. Simpkins comments how *Giant Steps* is "awesome in the technical proficiency shown, the tight mathematical logic behind the compositions, the utilization of ideas such as ostinato, pedal point, the extensive use of minor thirds instead of the traditional fourth or halfstep." It was the first time Coltrane expressed his ideas on an entire album, the first time that he seriously attempted to create, like Monk, his own musical architecture.

The compositions are meticulously constructed, possessing a stunningly logical symmetry. Examining and dissecting them is similar to examining the inner workings of a fine Swiss watch. The title piece from *Giant Steps* and "Countdown" from *Coltrane Jazz* advance many of the Davis ideas in attempting to free themselves from the restrictions of harmony.

"Giant Steps" had been worked on as early as 1956 and contains a modulating pattern which moves from minor thirds to fourths. As Bill Cole notes, it offers a remarkable example of "just how fluent Trane could be, bouncing and moving through the European harmonic system which he had mastered so well" and containing musical ideas moving in "both arpeggios and scale lines" at the same time. Along with "Naima," this piece would become the most played of his compositions. "Countdown" is another masterful creation of logical symmetry which elaborates on the Miles Davis composition "Tune Up." Like "Giant Steps" it also moves from minor thirds to fourths. Both "Countdown" and "Giant Steps" lay a solid foundation for later compositions such as "Impressions," "Chasin' the Trane," and those from *A Love Supreme*.

While "Giant Steps" and "Countdown" achieve their moods basically through a constant movement or modulation between chords, "Naima" from *Giant Steps* achieves a hauntingly reflective mood through an overlay, rather than a movement, of chords. As Coltrane once said about the piece, "It's built on suspended chords over an Eb pedal tone on the outside. On the inside...the chords are suspended over a Bb pedal tone." The mixture of the tonic and dominant creates a drone-like sound, and it is from this drone that the improvisations are created.

The use of a continuous pedal tone and the creation of a drone sound are significant elements of Indian music and represent parts of a certain sound that Coltrane had been attempting to approximate since he had first heard it during his withdrawal from drugs in 1957. It was a mysterious sound to Coltrane like the sounds of a city in the early morning hours. Coltrane once observed it was like holding a seashell to his ear.

However one describes the strange sound, it contained some essential truth for him, existing as an omnipresent background hum behind the facade of everyday life. In a sense it was cosmic music and he suspected it might open doors into new areas of perception and future worlds only imagined in his wildest dreams. Yet it was also an ancient sound passed down through the centuries by small schools of esoteric musicians. Because it was an ancient sound and had many non-Western elements in it, Coltrane suspected its origin was the Middle East or India.

In a sense, the search for this mysterious sound would become Coltrane's attempt to discover his own Holy Grail. Like the sound itself, his search for the sound was in the background of much of his sixties work and would provide a stimulus for innovative works such as "India" and "My Favorite Things." With "Naima" the search for the mysterious sound was just getting underway.

Another interesting composition from this period is "Harmonique" from *Coltrane Jazz*. More than anything else, it demonstrates Coltrane's increasing desire to explore tonal centers and investigate the sounds connected with a specific pitch. Bill Cole notes that "The harmonic is actually the tone or tones connected in the overtone series of any specific note. For instance, if a person strikes an A on a tuning fork the sound that is produced is not only an A but all the sounds that are connected with that specific pitch." With "Harmonique" Coltrane began to seriously explore the various tones connected with a pitch.

This exploration led to greater improvisational freedom and is later evidenced on a number of recordings from the mid-sixties. The new technique would help him escape a linear form of improvisation to a more circular form. It would allow him to orbit a certain sound, attempting new juxtapositions of that sound, seeing the sound from many perspectives and angles. In a sense, the technique was similar to the school of modern art known as Cubism, for Coltrane, as painters such as Picasso attempted in their work, was interested in examining life from different angles. Understanding his relationship to certain tonal centers allowed Coltrane to pursue new dimensions in jazz improvisation during the sixties in the context of the John Coltrane Quartet.

As he moved into a new decade, the new plateau gave

him a vantage point to see the possibilities of music in the hazy distance. For the first time in his life, he believed that it might be possible to accomplish his musical and philosophical goals, to one day approximate the strange sound he was hearing.

If he had tried to examine the terrain of his future musical travels from that plateau he might have seen some storm clouds over the distant mountains. But this was not his style in his music or in his life. He believed in that instantaneous spark of time called the present where the future transformed itself into the past. These fleeting moments in time when he saw things in new perspectives were the most insightful glimpses into new modes of perception. He felt the musician must be ready to pursue them wherever they might lead. But to fully take advantage of the possibilities in these moments one had to be intensely involved in the present. One had to be more concerned with examining the immediate ground around oneself on that ridge of life than in looking far off into the distance for future storm clouds. He was in awe from what he saw around him.

In one of her more surrealist passages, the author Anaïs Nin describes a certain character saying, "His gaze came from the remotest worlds of light and silence, piercing through our exterior, exposing instantly the naked soul and remaining there before the exposure, full of surprise, wonder and awe." It was the type of gaze John Coltrane possessed after recording *Giant Steps* and *Coltrane Jazz*.

The view from this artistic summit, though, despite its

awesome and majestic beauty, was still a personal one, a Tolkienesque kingdom existing solely within the geography of an individual mind, and much of Coltrane's energy during the next few years, the early years of the sixties, would be directed toward finding the most effective method to communicate this view to others.

In some ways, as Nat Hentoff sees these years, it was a time of introspection and reflection for Coltrane. On the liner notes to *The Coltrane Legacy*, recorded in 1960, he writes it was a time of "a consolidating of skills, a gentling time of comparative simplicity and immediately assailable clarity of line and form" containing a "pervasive relaxation" in the music which reminded one of "how much gentleness Coltrane could give." Pieces such as "Centerpiece" and "Untitled Original" off the *Legacy* album have a cheerful, Sunday-picnic, laid-back feeling.

However, the period was not completely dominated by peacefulness and relaxation in Coltrane's music. This becomes evident with pieces such as "Impressions," "India," "Spiritual" and "Chasin' the Trane" from 1961, which evidence few of the qualities of "pervasive relaxation" Hentoff finds in *The Coltrane Legacy* album. If anything they are near the other extreme.

More than anything else it was a period of experimentation to find an essential style, a particular context to give Coltrane's inner visions a powerful outward expression. He was continuing his study of Eastern music and had taken to playing a new instrument, the soprano saxophone, in order to get an eastern sound. In 1961, this

Eastern music was presented on *Olé Coltrane* and *Africa/Brass.*

If he was looking toward Eastern music for a particular sound, he was beginning to concentrate on African music as a possible container for the rhythm of this sound. In the September 29, 1960, issue of *Down Beat* Coltrane observes that "I want to be more flexible where rhythm is concerned," and "I feel I have to study rhythm some more...I haven't experimented too much with time...most of my experimenting has been in a harmonic form...I put time and rhythms to one side, in the past."

Initial findings of African rhythm as a container for this sound would be the composition "Africa" from *Africa/Brass.* As the sixties progressed, these rhythm experiments would get more and more bizarre as he became increasingly preoccupied with rhythm, almost exclusively, toward the end of his life.

Bursts of creative energy continued during this period. In November 1961, his close friend Eric Dolphy joined him at New York's Village Vanguard. In May and June of 1961, *Africa/Brass* and *Olé Coltrane* were recorded. Overall, though, it was a period of experimentation which bore many interesting new concepts and ideas but relatively little fruit. Atlantic reissued a number of his earlier works, including *The Best of John Coltrane, The Art of John Coltrane* and *The Coltrane Legacy,* to promote one of their artists who had temporarily slowed his output of original compositions. As he writes in the *Down Beat* article from this time, "I want to get the material first. Right now, I'm on a material search."

That he was searching for material and not creating tells us much about the core of his experiments during this period. The extended solo had never been so thoroughly explored in the history of jazz. To Coltrane, who would often launch into hour-long solos during club dates, a composition was not the container for the sound he was attempting to achieve but rather a launching pad for a vast spontaneous exploration of the sound. The composition was no longer an extended exercise in dancing through advanced European harmonics, such as "Giant Steps" and "Countdown," but rather a preliminary piece to do little more than define the ground from which Coltrane would launch musical ideas.

During the early sixties he makes long treks into the outer reaches of the world of sound. While on these treks the overall structure of a seven-or eight-minute composition is of little interest to him. In certain respects he is like Kurtz from Conrad's famous story "Heart of Darkness" as he pursues musical visions up long, winding rivers of his mind. At times, the visions become an obsession and he is oblivious to the audience as he chases them with his horn for upward of an hour.

However, this was not the music which created successful records, so his record company was forced to tread water in the interim until their star could get back to making commercially successful works such as *Giant Steps* and *Coltrane Jazz*. For Atlantic this time never came and *Olé Coltrane*, recorded in May 1961, was his last association with them before being signed by Impulse, the record label he would stay with the rest of his life.

Impulse understood Coltrane and seldom questioned the value of recording solos which often took the entire side of a record. Unlike past labels who were content to simply capture the "studio" Coltrane, Impulse sought to capture the wildly furious Coltrane in the electrifying atmosphere of smoky, live club dates.

The first Impulse date was November 1961, and resulted in *Coltrane Live At The Village Vanguard*. It was the beginning of an association with an incredible group of recording people such as Impulse producer Bob Thiele and an amazing technical wizard named Rudy Van Gelder, owner of the famous Van Gelder Recording Studio outside of New York City. Through the relentless efforts of Thiele and Van Gelder to capture Coltrane's long experiments on record, we are left with the most important work of Coltrane's career.

Summons

The final element in his experiments of the early sixties was finding the right musicians to bring it all together. For a deeply spiritual person like Coltrane, now possessed by the need to communicate a musical vision, this element was the most important.

He needed superb musicians; there was never a question about this. He needed people who had, like him, learned under other jazz masters, and who knew their instruments so well that they were like appendages. But even more, he needed musicians who could keep pace with his growth, who could help him reach some of the new plateaus he saw opening before him. He needed fellow travelers along the path, soulmates in the odyssey he was about to begin. In some respects, he needed disciples to help him spread the message he was beginning to hear, to help him find the strange sound he had been hearing in his head.

This combination proved elusive, and he would search desperately to find it. The search began in 1959 after *Giant Steps* and continued into 1961 when *Live At The Village Vanguard* was recorded. In the process he would play for extended periods of time with superb musicians such as bassists Charlie Haden, Reggie Workman, Art Davis and

Steve Davis, or drummers Billy Higgins and Jimmy Cobb, all excellent musicians and masters of their craft but not what he was searching for.

After leaving Miles Davis in 1960 to go on his own, Coltrane was soon approached by the old owners of the Five Spot where the legendary Monk encounter had taken place. He was given an offer hard to refuse. Joe and Iggy Termini now owned a new jazz club called the Jazz Gallery, and they promised to pay Coltrane the same salary that Davis had paid him to play for twenty weeks at their club. The offer was too good to refuse because it would allow him to play for an extended period of time with his own group. It was an opportunity which had never presented itself to him, and it was an opportunity which he had never been prepared to pursue.

This was what he had been dreaming about. He might finally become a leader. He accepted the Termini offer and began to assemble his group. His close friend Sonny Rollins suggested Pete La Rocca, a drummer who had played with him. For bassist he chose an old friend from Philadelphia, Steve Davis. He had first met his wife Naima in Steve's house in June of 1954. For pianist he chose a young musician named Steve Kuhn, an Ivy League-educated white pianist. Kuhn had called Coltrane out of the blue one day and told him that he thought he could "contribute" to Coltrane's music. Coltrane was in a bind because the pianist he wanted was not immediately available and the Termini offer necessitated immediate action.

After a preliminary review of Kuhn's excellent musical

credentials, he agreed to meet him in a rehearsal studio. They played together for a few hours and Coltrane called Kuhn two days later and asked him to join him for his opening at the Jazz Gallery. Kuhn agreed, and the first John Coltrane Quartet opened there in May of 1960.

The Jazz Gallery, a large club, was packed on that warm May evening for Coltrane's appearance with his new group. A feeling of great expectation was in the air at the club among the interesting mixture of people in the audience, including intellectuals, termed "beatniks" at the time, avant-garde writers and painters, and the hard-core jazz fans. And, of course, other musicians who came to see the results of something many of them had been urging Coltrane to do. Pianist Cecil Taylor sat in the balcony and the legendary Thelonious Sphere Monk was at the front waiting for the music.

When it started, wild excitement erupted in the club and one member of the audience, a large bald-headed black man wearing nothing but a loincloth, ran up the aisle shouting, "Coltrane! Coltrane! Coltrane!" Following him, and doing a funny little dance, was none other than Monk. The next day the opening performance got a rave review in the *New York Daily News* which said "Run, do not walk or otherwise loiter on your way down to the Jazz Gallery (to hear) John Coltrane...who has the future coming out of his horn."

In spite of the enthusiastic opening, Coltrane was not satisfied with the sound. In some ways, the rhythm section seemed to be competing with instead of supporting him.

And with Kuhn this problem was only magnified. After some serious thought he decided that it was time to contact the pianist he had admired since the mid-fifties when he heard him at the Red Rooster Club in Philadelphia. The pianist was McCoy Tyner.

During those early years in Philadelphia the young Tyner, a phenomenal eighteen-year-old piano player in his own right, used to visit Coltrane often and the two would sit on Coltrane's porch for hours and talk about music and life. Tyner recalls that it wasn't that he was convinced by Coltrane's ideas but rather that it seemed that "we had sort of a consistency there, we coincided."

Coltrane told Tyner during this time that whenever he got his own group together he wanted him to join. He was with Miles Davis at the time, though, so this was not an immediate possibility. Tyner was not able to wait until this happened. He was offered the piano spot in a group fronted by Benny Golson, the hard bop tenorist from Philadelphia. It was too good an offer to refuse and Tyner joined Golson at a gig in San Francisco. When they returned to New York, trumpeter Art Farmer joined them and the group became the Jazztet.

The Jazztet had an almost immediate popularity and Tyner found himself playing with them at the Village Vanguard during the same time Coltrane's first group was playing at the Jazz Gallery. During the breaks, Tyner would run over to hear Coltrane. It made Coltrane feel good to see McCoy and he wanted to ask the young Tyner to join in Kuhn's spot but did not want to take him away from his old friend Benny Golson whom he had also grown up with in Philadelphia. And Tyner, being only twenty years old, had trouble telling Golson that he wanted to quit.

Naima finally intervened. She told her husband that if he wanted McCoy to join his group he had better ask him. He did and Tyner accepted. It was one of the happiest days in Tyner's life, the fulfillment of a desire he had carried since those long discussions on the Coltrane porch back in Philadelphia. For Coltrane, it was a very happy day also. He gave notice to Steve Kuhn, and soon McCoy Tyner was in the piano spot.

For the next few years there would be more testing and experiments to find the correct combination of musicians, but Tyner would never be replaced. He became a Rock of Gibraltar for these initial efforts, an anchor keeping the music on center. He would stay with Coltrane on virtually all of his important work through 1965, when Coltrane would finally replace him with his wife Alice Coltrane.

Born in Philadelphia on December 11, 1938, Tyner had grown up in a rich musical environment which included the legendary pianist Bud Powell as a neighbor. The two became good friends, with Powell becoming the first major influence on his career. He rounded out the direct education he was getting from Powell with intense practice and lessons in most of Philadelphia's finer musical institutions. He was heavily influenced by the great classical composers, as Coltrane was. He especially liked the music of Debussy and had a large collection of his records.

In the mid-fifties, Tyner began working with a number of important young stars around Philadelphia like Sonny Rollins, Clifford Brown, Bud Powell's brother Richie Powell, Kenny Dorham, and trumpeter Cal Massey and Massey's band. In a few years, Benny Golson offered him the job in what would become the Jazztet.

This group, led by Art Farmer and Benny Golson, was one of the finest hard-bop units of the late fifties. Golson was an alumnus of the Gillespie band of the mid-fifties who went on to play with one of the original hard-bop groups, Art Blakey's Jazz Messengers. His style on tenor, though, had more than the biting sharpness of the hard-bop tenorists. It had a warm lyricism, a softer ballad-like tone characteristic of Coleman Hawkins, Don Byas and Ben Webster's styles of the thirties.

Trumpeter Art Farmer, the Jazztet's other leader, possessed one of the most lyrical sounds in all of modern jazz. As Joachim Berendt notes, Farmer was one of the very few who could "equal the lyrical intensity of Davis without imitating Miles." Like Golson, Farmer also had experience playing with hard-driving boppers. In the early fifties he joined Lionel Hampton's band and went with them to Europe, where he recorded an album with the legendary trumpeter Clifford Brown entitled *Clifford Brown Memorial*. Brown, probably more than anyone else, was the real father of the hard-bop school. Leaving Hampton and Brown, Farmer played with a wide variety of jazz greats such as Sonny Rollins, Horace Silver and the respected visionary modal composer George Russell.

The Jazztet's mixture of hard-driving jazz with strongly melodic phrasing provided a unique musical environment for the young Tyner. It was one of the few groups in jazz to suggest a synthesis of the cool lyricism of Miles Davis and the hot power of Art Blakey and Clifford Brown. And it was perhaps the only group that really effectively implemented this synthesis.

With McCoy Tyner at piano, Coltrane finally had the basic foundation he was searching for. Unlike the out-front, argumentative style of Kuhn, a style that had often placed Kuhn in competition with Coltrane as they traded solos at the Jazz Gallery, Tyner's style had an elegant, majestic quality and a powerful lyricism. He was one of the few modern jazz pianists successfully experimenting in improvisation based on tonal centers and various modes.

In a sense Tyner interpreted what Miles Davis was doing with his horn in highly modal experiments such as *Kind Of Blue* and placed them in a piano context. Moods were suggested in the eloquent style of Tyner, certain musical centers hinted at but never fully defined. It was highly evocative, setting up rich and thickly textured musical landscapes above which Coltrane could soar. His amazing left hand seemingly roamed at will up and down the keyboard while suggesting certain musical plateaus or levels, a certain "higher ground" from which Coltrane could again improvise.

Coltrane and Tyner produced one of the most dynamic interactions in the history of jazz. It was a subtle interaction, though, never possessing the back-and-forth trade-off of jazz soloing as it had been practiced in the past. Rather it was an interaction which often coincided so well, meshed so precisely, that it was impossible to even distinguish the two interacting forces. They were simply one.

This new, powerful duo jazz voice is evident from the beginning. During the summer of 1960, Tyner is first heard on record with Coltrane in *Echoes Of An Era*. It is one of Coltrane's lesser-known works and came right in the middle of his search to find the remaining two musicians for the rhythm section. Although there is some solid backing from Steve Davis on bass and Billy Higgins on drums on pieces such as "Exotica" and "One and Four," it is a far cry from the type of musical interaction that Tyner and Coltrane evidence on this album.

The search to find the proper bassist and drummer continued through the summer of 1960. In July 1960, Coltrane recorded an album with Don Cherry, one of the prime forces of the emerging Ornette Coleman-inspired "free jazz" school of musicians who would become so important in the sixties. Apart from the importance of this exposure of Coltrane to these radical new musical ideas, the album is tentative because he has yet to find the right combination of musicians to communicate his inner vision to the world. This combination and interaction was of prime importance and it does not happen on *The Avant-Garde* with Cherry. Charlie Haden on bass and Ed Blackwell on drums provide solid backing, but like Steve Davis and Billy Higgins on the earlier *Echoes Of An Era*, they lack the punch Coltrane was looking for.

Three months later, in October 1960, Coltrane made an album which finally realized the interaction he had been searching for. Tyner was on piano, Davis was back on bass and Elvin Jones was on drums. The album was *My Favorite Things* and it sold more than 50,000 copies during its first year of release, making it one of the most popular jazz albums in history. More than any other album it brought Coltrane a wider audience of listeners and won him the number one spot on tenor saxophone in the famous *Down Beat* magazine poll, the first time Coltrane occupied this spot.

The song, a simple lyrical waltz in three-quarter time written by the well-known Broadway team of Rogers and Hammerstein, provided Coltrane the perfect vehicle to explore and test some of his ideas. Uppermost in his mind was a fascination with Eastern music and his feeling that the best way to enter its exotic and mysterious world was by the extended jazz solo.

After an initial statement of the theme by the group, Coltrane enters on the high register of the soprano sax sounding more like an Indian snake charmer than a jazz musician. The horn's sound is definitely something new and unique in jazz. The only other tenorist even closely approximating it was Coltrane's old friend and teacher, Yusef Lateef. Sounding at times like the moans of some great caged spirit, its tone is harsh, at times possessing an eerie, chant-like underpinning, a drone never explicitly stated in the melody or rhythm but always buzzing some-where behind or through the music. The listener feels the presence of this strange sound more than actually hearing the sound. It is almost like some shadowy presence lurking above the music, watching over the event, and any attempts to define this presence only cause the sound to quickly go scurrying away. One must go by feeling alone to know whether it is there or not—the processes of thinking about it and analyzing it are inadequate.

As the piece progresses, the group reaches for higher and higher ground. Plateaus are reached and new terrain quickly sketched by the musicians, and then Coltrane again soars above the plateau searching for even higher resting points. In this upward musical flight, Coltrane depends on Tyner to define the plateaus and on Davis to make sure that they steadily progress toward them.

He depended on his new drummer, Elvin Jones, to help him explore his new interest in rhythm. As he admitted in the September 29, 1960, issue of *Down Beat*, "I haven't experimented too much with time," and that in the past he had "put time and rhythms to one side." He felt strongly during this period of his life that he should give most of his musical attention to that substance from the fourth dimension called time, spoken about so eloquently by Albert Einstein, one of his greatest heroes.

His past triumphs had been in the harmonic form for the most part. After brilliant harmonic explorations such as *Giant Steps* and after prophetic understanding of new modal ways of stating the melody evidenced on *Kind Of Blue*, there was not much further to immediately go in these two areas. Rhythm was the next logical idea to pursue for Coltrane after these albums.

He had an idea of what he wanted. At times he could hear the thunder in his head, the drone he had heard in his room in 1957. Coltrane concluded that rhythm had much to do with the strange magical qualities of the drone and he felt it must be pursued with all of his energy and strength. Coltrane was not searching for the traditional form of rhythm which swing music had introduced and which was now prevalent. This form had the jazz drummer keeping the main pulse of the beat with his left foot on the bass drum while riding his high-hat cymbal and punctuating every now and then with short attacks on his snare drums. Coltrane was looking for something far different.

He reached some tentative conclusions. Perhaps the drums should be given a broader function than merely keeping rhythm. Perhaps they should have a more melodic than rhythmic function. It was a relatively new idea to the early sixties jazz scene. However, it was not totally novel. In fact, taking a sweeping view of jazz history, one can see that the drums were breaking away from their earlier role as a carrier for the melody and harmony and evolving toward a melodic instrument.

The evolution intensified tremendously during the forties when bop became the prevalent jazz style. Kenny Clarke, more than any other bop drummer, was at the center of this intensity. Clarke was the original house drummer at the famous Minton's in the late forties and was largely responsible for drumming bop music into existence and inspiring a freer rhythmic conception for the drums.

The traditional meter, carried in the past by the bass drum and the high-hat cymbal, ceased to exist for Clarke, who began using his drums for accents and punctuation as much as for rhythm. In the fifties Max Roach would extend Clarke's original concepts of polyrhythmic accompaniment within the context of the brilliant Max Roach-Clifford Brown quintet. The main beat shifted from the bass drum to the cymbals. The rest of the drums were then used to accent subsidiary rhythms and counterpoints to the soloist.

In the early sixties Elvin Jones further extended the Clarke and Roach ideas and Coltrane was well aware of this fact. But more than seeing Jones as the carrier of a unique rhythmic torch in jazz, Coltrane knew about the historical importance of the drums to the African people. During this period he was intensely involved with studying African music, and from this study certain ideas were becoming clear to him.

Central to his findings about African music, he came to realize that rhythm played the dominant role. He also discovered that African music was inseparable from other areas of African society, rhythm pervaded all of African society.

Coltrane was feeling the power and beauty of his heritage for the first time in his life and was intent on knowing all he could about the history of the large and mysterious continent of Africa. It was a history that Coltrane came to realize was transmitted through rhythm more than words or any other musical device. He concluded that rhythm might be the most effective way to explore African history. It could provide a direct historical link to powerful periods in African history.

One of the greatest periods in African history occurred during the twelfth and thirteenth centuries when the great Mali Empire was established under King Sundiata Keita and King Mansu Musa. King Sundiata was banished from the kingdom of Mali by his brother and lived in exile for a number of years. Around 1230, the people of Mali sent a messenger to Sundiata asking him to return and rule the kingdom. Upon his return he established the great unification of African states under the Empire of Mali. When King Musa ascended to the throne in 1307, he found a strong and well-organized empire. During King Musa's reign much of the wealthy land of the Niger River basin and key trading cities such as Timbuktu were brought under the control of the Mali Empire. And, under Musa's reign a significant event in African history was the growth of the Moslem religion in North Africa, which culminated in the great pilgrimage to Mecca in 1324.

In many ways it was the African counterpart to the European Renaissance. But unlike the outpouring of creative effort in Italy which left thousands of artifacts behind, the African Renaissance of the Mali Empire left little visible evidence behind. Only a memory of this beautiful period of African history remained, but this memory was strong and passed down through generations by Griots, master musicians of the villages. Usually the oldest members of their villages, the Griots devoted their lives to learning and memorizing an elaborate set of rhythms which spoke of the great Mali period of African history. Communication was not through words or melodies but rather solely through rhythms. The Griots were African historians, keepers of the Malian memory.

In a sense, Coltrane was a modern-day Griot. Each day he was becoming more aware of this magnificent history, each day feeling more part of it and deriving more power from it. It was a memory forgotten by most African Americans. And, for Coltrane, it was a memory difficult to summon through the haze of narcotic fogs holding him captive in the early fifties.

But now this memory was coming to him like a slow movie fade-in until he could begin to experience the feeling of living in the golden period of African history. Slowly he was gaining access to the inner sanctum of Africa's musical heritage. In a large sense, it is Africa's heritage to the world. He alone among jazz musicians was beginning to stare into what some might term the "collective unconscious" of the African culture.

Was he being permitted to do this by some great spiritual force, or was he himself creating this feeling for African history? It was an extremely important question to Coltrane, a question he would spend the rest of his life attempting to answer through his music.

In the early 1960s he was convinced that rhythm was the best way to explore this inner sanctum. And the more he moved into an exploration of rhythm, the more he became convinced he needed a master of rhythm to accompany him on his journey of exploration. He needed someone close to these original rhythms, a direct link to the ancient Griot methods, someone who possessed some of the secrets of the great heritage. He needed someone to speak to him with rhythm and to push him toward the archetypes of the African sound. He needed a counterpoint to his ideas, a source of energy to provide a constant flow of fuel for his solo flights.

He had known for some time that he needed Elvin Jones. Born in 1927 into an amazing musical family which included brothers Hank and Thad Jones, Elvin had worked out some of his developing concepts of a freer rhythmic style in the context of the classic Sonny Rollins trio of the fifties. On *A Night At The Village Vanguard* Jones can be heard juxtaposing his polyrhythmic accompaniment against the powerful tenor of Rollins. At times sparks fly from the juxtaposition, but it is evident that Jones is spilling over with rhythmic ideas. Breaking away from the traditional jazz pulse, he launched a barrage of accents and patterns which offered the soloist an endless source of possibilities.

Coltrane needed Jones from when he had first thought of organizing his own group. Unfortunately, though, Jones was temporarily detained in an all-too-worldly establishment run by the federal government called Rikers Island. He was in for a drug bust.

It was the summer of 1960, and Coltrane was having problems with his current drummer, Pete LaRoca. The early Coltrane quartet, with Tyner on piano and Steve Davis on bass, was on tour, and after playing at a place called the Minor Key in Detroit, Coltrane gave LaRoca his walking papers. LaRoca was an excellent drummer, but his style and rhythmic conception were simply too far removed from Coltrane's.

He then got in touch with Billy Higgins, who had been working in Los Angeles with Ornette Coleman, and arranged to use him on drums when the group arrived in Los Angeles, their next stop. However, after one rehearsal Coltrane realized that Higgins was not right either. As J.C. Thomas notes in *Chasin' The Trane*, "Where LaRoca played behind the beat, Higgins was right on top of it."

Somewhat coincidentally, Coltrane met Elvin's brother Thad Jones while in Los Angeles. Thad told him that Elvin was just getting out of jail and gave him a number where the drummer could be reached. After Coltrane called New York several times each day trying to reach Elvin, he finally reached him and Jones immediately told Coltrane that of course he would enjoy playing with him. It was the most exciting opportunity of his life.

Coltrane flew Elvin to Denver, the next engagement on their tour, and when Elvin arrived at the club in Denver he found a new set of drums waiting for him on the bandstand, courtesy of Coltrane. As bassist Steve Davis recalls, "That first night Elvin was in the band, he was playing so strong and so loud you could hear him outside the club and down the block...Elvin was one of the strongest, wildest drummers in the world." Davis remembers how after the performance that evening, "Trane put his arm around Elvin, took him to a barbecue place around the corner, and bought him some ribs." Davis adds that "Trane and Elvin were tight from then on."

A few months later in October of 1960, the Coltrane quartet with Elvin Jones on drums made its first appearance on record with *My Favorite Things*. Much has been said and written about the album: how it was the prime reason for the growing popularity of the quartet, how it sold 50,000 copies (a "million seller" in the jazz community), and how it launched Coltrane and the quartet into exploration of the extended jazz solo. This is all true, but sometimes can distract from the amazing interplay between Coltrane and Jones on the title piece, "My Favorite Things."

It was an interplay which marked a unique new concept in jazz, a concept recently surfacing from the New York underground where it had existed for years. It was a concept which could be heard blaring out of Ornette Coleman's garage in Los Angeles. Later in the sixties the concept would become the most influential in jazz. It would have an entire school of musicians built around it, and the school's founders would be John Coltrane and Ornette Coleman.

It would be called Free Jazz.

Freedom

Previously jazz tradition dictated that only one player should improvise at a time. One member would play the role of star while the others became the supporting cast. The structure of the group, the inner dynamics of three, four or five people working creatively together to make something more than all of them, had not been adequately examined in the past.

John Coltrane and Ornette Coleman challenged the assumption that a jazz group should possess only one star. They saw a jazz group as something composed of a number of stars who should solo whenever they wanted. The guiding light behind their concept was that a certain creative power could come from spontaneous group interaction. It was the antithesis of Duke Ellington's meticulously composed music and led to some rather bizarre happenings. Listening to some of the later free jazz groups is like standing in the middle of a barnyard full of frenzied animals: pigs honking, cows moaning and hens squawking as everyone does their own thing.

It was a period of brotherhood and equality in American history when people asked why one person in a group should be more important than another. In this manner, politics came to influence jazz music structure. But politics was never a real concern to John Coltrane and Ornette Coleman. While both were involved in the growing civil rights movement, they were really above politics. Their central idea was that the group's sound should give each member inspiration, and that each member should express this inspiration whenever appropriate. Like most political ideas, it was a vague rallying cry for people who felt the same way on some things but not on others. Coleman and Coltrane went beyond the idea of brotherhood for the sake of brotherhood and came to examine the relationship itself and not the label placed on it. They asked if members of the relationship were adding positive forces to the group. This was the overriding question, and Coltrane answered with a resounding "Yes!" on the title cut from *My Favorite Things* in October of 1960; he had found that positive force he had been searching for in Elvin Jones.

"My Favorite Things" by the early Coltrane quartet has not been considered an example of the emerging free jazz movement. The music seems too melodic to be part of this chaotic new music. However, if one listens to the Coltrane-Jones interaction on the October 21, 1960, recording of "My Favorite Things" (and there would be a number of recordings) one can hear free jazz played superbly by Coltrane and Jones. Later, on albums such as *Ascension*, free jazz would be played by all group members. On *My Favorite Things*, though, the original idea of a strong interaction between musicians within an improvisational context is clearly and beautifully stated between Coltrane and Jones.

It was at the core of the music Coltrane would contribute to the free jazz movement.

On the title cut, the tenorist and drummer exchange a barrage of musical ideas and questions, each one continually throwing unique harmonic and rhythmic juxtapositions against each other, creating a powerful new jazz sound not based on melody or rhythm but on a relationship between the musicians. Throughout the extended exchange of ideas, it is often impossible to discern with which musician the ideas originate. A polyrhythmic Jones off on the drums will suggest something to Coltrane, who will extend these rhythms with his horn and carry them a little further and higher like a musical baton being passed to him in a relay race. Then something Coltrane does will inspire Jones and the baton will be temporarily passed back.

The direct musical confrontations on "My Favorite Things," though, do not extend to Tyner and Davis. There is interaction but it is subtle, pervading the atmosphere so well, creating the atmosphere to a certain extent, that it goes mostly unnoticed. More than anything else it is their task to sketch the general landscape for the Coltrane-Jones encounters, to splash dabs of color onto the musical painting. Davis' bass moves the group forward, a function entrusted to him almost alone now since Jones is off soloing against Coltrane. He provides the final tether for the group, as tenuous as it is at times, to the meter of the composition. Tyner, on the other hand, works not so much on momentum as on foundation. More than anyone else, Tyner defines the general musical level these group interactions will take place on. It is Tyner who magically levitates the performing platform skyward.

In the overall interaction of the group on "My Favorite Things," Coltrane keeps pulling energy toward him like some musical black hole. His high-register playing sounds like the moaning of an animal at times, but it is a powerful moaning, containing many new ideas from Eastern music. The moaning, chant-like sound Coltrane gets from his saxophone then propels the group to new levels.

The process provides Coltrane with a way of extending former ideas and escaping the dilemma he often arrived at during his sheets of sound period of the fifties. During those years his improvisational flights were magnificent, but they often led into a musical stalemate or quicksand. His ideas blasted through his saxophone in this period at supersonic speed, but they far outdistanced the others and he found himself alone with no energy to draw on.

Now, though, his group was with him, supplying new energy for the Coltrane horn—especially Elvin. More than anyone else, Elvin beat Coltrane out of his past dilemmas and stalemates, feeding 100,000 volts to him like a portable nuclear reactor, pushing his horn playing into new areas of spontaneous music. With the addition of Jones, he almost had the nucleus he was searching for.

Almost.

Toward the end of 1960, Coltrane was spending a number of his evenings at a small jazz club in Greenwich Village listening to an exciting bass player named Reggie Workman. Since Workman was from Philadelphia, Coltrane knew his work. But now, teamed up with a strong drummer named Roy Haynes, Workman was pushing his bass into new areas Coltrane had not heard. Coltrane sat at the club and listened intently to Workman.

In early 1961, Coltrane took Davis aside after an engagement in Philadelphia and quietly told him, like Kuhn a few months before, he was going to make a change; Davis was out and Workman in. Davis remembers that "Reggie had really developed. I think he was coming on stronger, playing more up front than I was. I know some people were telling John they couldn't hear the bass. Maybe this influenced his decision, but I'm not sure."

The strong Workman bass is first heard on record with Coltrane in May of 1961 on *Africa/Brass* and *Olé Coltrane*. However, on both of these albums Coltrane uses a unique new combination of two bass players. Along with Workman he uses bassist Art Davis. The simultaneous bass playing of Workman and Davis approximates the mysterious drone sound Coltrane first heard in 1957 and is best exemplified on "Africa" from *Africa/Brass*. As Coltrane states on the album's liner notes, "I wanted the band to have a drone...One bass plays it almost all the way through. The other has rhythmic lines around it."

It was a brilliant and largely successful experiment by Coltrane to re-create that sound he had heard in 1957, attempting to break away from heroin addiction. It was also a brilliant exploration of his increasing interest in African history and its ancient tribal rhythms, offering a new environment for his interaction with Elvin Jones.

Still, something was missing in the overall group sound. At the Village Vanguard in November of 1961, he again used two bass players. Art Davis was out and Reggie Workman now played with bassist Jimmy Garrison. With Garrison, Coltrane's search for the right group ends.

As McCoy Tyner recalls, "I don't remember exactly why Reggie left, but I'll say this about Jimmy, his time and choice of notes was the best of all the bass players John used." And Coltrane had used many talented bass players since breaking out with *Giant Steps*. The list includes musicians Charlie Haden, Percy Heath and Paul Chambers. His long search to find the bass sound he wanted says much about the music he was creating, his constantly changing rhythmic conceptions and his search for the strange drone sound. And over the course of his search, Coltrane's ideas about the bass changed as his solos got longer and longer.

One thing about the bass function seemed clear to him—the bass would play an auxiliary part supplying energy to the two soloists on the front line of the battle. Tyner remembers that Garrison "stayed more in the background, and that was what John really wanted."

But Garrison did more than stay in the background during the next five years; he created the background. And significantly, Garrison, unlike Tyner and Jones, would stay with Coltrane to the end. On Coltrane's last recording, *Expression*, from early 1967, Alice Coltrane is on piano, Rashied Ali is on drums, Pharoah Sanders is on sax and piccolo, and Jimmy Garrison is on bass. During those five years, especially 1965, the front line of the group changed a number of times but the background bass always remained.

In November 1961, the full John Coltrane Quartet finally came together in two amazing recording dates which are arguably the finest of his career. One was a live recording, *Coltrane Live At The Village Vanguard*, and the other was *Impressions*. For a few years the powerful spiritual force of Coltrane had acted like a great cosmic gravitational field pulling members of the group together around him. Now the group exploded outward like a musical super-nova with the *Vanguard* and the *Impressions* dates. The initial explosion started in May with the brilliant *Africa/Brass* and *Olé Coltrane* recording dates, and now they pushed that high plateau even higher to one of the peaks in Coltrane's career.

The title cut from *Impressions* is an updated restatement of the modes originally explored in the tune "So What" from the landmark Davis album *Kind Of Blue*. Borrowing an opening melody from Debussy, "Impressions" punches out at the listener with a strong reworking of the Debussy line. And the stunning tribute to the East on "India" from *Impressions* represents Coltrane's first recorded acknowledgment of the importance of Indian music to him.

Although *Impressions* was not released until 1963, both the title cut and "India" were recorded during those few historic evenings at the Village Vanguard in November of 1961. It was a high-energy peak in Coltrane's career. On November 2 and 3 the people from Coltrane's new Impulse label were there to record the last set of each evening. Their work resulted in the first extended live recordings of the new Coltrane group. Bob Thiele supervised the original recordings and Rudy Van Gelder was the recording engineer. It followed the brilliant first effort of Impulse on *Africa/Brass* and evidenced the label's strong support of Coltrane and their desire to record the "club" Coltrane as opposed to the "studio" Coltrane.

The two Coltranes were contrasts, their differences becoming increasingly apparent. One of Coltrane's central ideas was the extended jazz solo and where it might lead. The saxophonist was just beginning to explore the possibilities in 1961 and very little could yet be said about the new land awaiting him over the next musical peak. Although Coltrane had no view of the new land, it seemed important to the Impulse people to present the search for it on record. The traditional studio setting, with its cold white linoleum flooring and fluorescent lighting made Coltrane nervous. The problem was intensified as he moved further and further into pure spontaneous compositions during the early sixties. The studio, with its outrageous demand that music be chopped into five-minute segments, was a problem Coltrane found hard to surmount. At clubs during this period he would often play an extended solo on his horn for upwards of an hour. How could he ever express this in a five-minute cut on an album?

He had been able to do this in 1959 with *Giant Steps*, but in a few short years he had journeyed far from the tightly structured compositions on that album, such as the title cut and "Countdown," to the spontaneous improvisation of "Chasin' the Trane" or "Spiritual" from the *Live At The Village Vanguard* date in late 1961. Perhaps it was another extreme in the seemingly perpetual mood swings throughout his life, a time when he was in total awe of life and attempted to express it all with his horn. In many respects it was similar to his sheets of sound period in the fifties with Miles Davis, another extreme period. Perhaps he had changed so much in a few years there is little sense in looking for past comparisons.

Whatever the case, it was apparent to many close to the heart of the avant-garde jazz scene that Coltrane's musical explorations were not going to fit neatly into seven or eight pieces for a standard jazz album. This was apparent to Bob Thiele at Impulse Records. The exploratory Coltrane of the smoky jazz clubs, the one causing wild excitement in the inner jazz community, this was the one to be captured on record, captured so that those who were not fortunate enough to attend the live performance might approximate the original experience.

Recording Coltrane live added additional fuel to a growing scrimmage between the Coltrane attackers and defenders. Many of Coltrane's Atlantic-label faithful admired the chord changes on masterpieces like "Giant Steps" or the straight-ahead strength demonstrated on pieces like "Some Other Blues" from *Coltrane Jazz* in the late 1950s. They could not understand the 1961 changes Coltrane was going through. These earlier Coltrane faithful had been brought to the music through the highly structured format of the ten Atlantic Coltrane albums and felt more comfortable with the old Atlantic Coltrane of the short, studio-recorded compositions.

It was a bold move by Impulse to record Coltrane at the Vanguard because the old Atlantic-label following translated into Coltrane's broad appeal. No one knew what would happen to this large following of the Atlantic "studio" Coltrane. He did have a club following, but only a certain number of people hear an artist on the club circuit. No matter how incredible the artist is in a "live" club setting, to really get his message out he has to go into the studio and record his work in short segments. Coltrane found this very difficult to do. His main concern was exploring the possibilities of extended jazz improvisation.

Few jazz labels at the time were willing to mutually explore this extended form of improvisation with their artists. Coming out of the cool jazz period of tightly structured and classically influenced "Europeanized" jazz, few labels could envision live, unstructured recording sessions which imposed few time restraints on the musicians. They wondered how they could ever market the music or get promotional airplay on radio stations with music that was ten or fifteen minutes long. As with all business enterprises, the record labels needed musical "products" to market. Few of them gave serious thought to the idea that the process of creating an artistic product might be a recordable product in itself.

Impulse was a relatively young, upstart medium-size jazz label which gave serious thought to the idea of recording live jazz in this initial post-cool jazz period. If it was difficult for the musicians to come into the studio, then Impulse would bring the studio to the musicians in the late night, low light, smoky environments of jazz clubs. It would be spontaneous for all involved. For the musicians, retakes, mixing and musical overlays were not possible, so their spontaneous thoughts would be recorded. For the record company, out of its natural habitat of the bright lights and fancy electronic buttons of the studio which sent the music through artificial transformations, it was also spontaneous. Someone in the club might trip over recording cords or spill a drink on the machine and an entire evening might be lost. In some ways, the live-recording labels were similar to early aviators who flew by the seat of their pants. They never knew exactly what music was around the next bend or whether it would lead toward some defined audience. It was a gamble.

Impulse decided to gamble in November of 1961 with the Vanguard recording date. They had gambled in their studios a few months earlier with *Africa/Brass*, the first of the long Coltrane studio albums they recorded. On side two of *Africa/Brass*, "Greensleeves" runs almost ten minutes and "Blues Minor" runs for over seven. And on side one the classic "Africa" stands alone and runs over sixteen minutes.

Recording engineer Rudy Van Gelder and producer Bob Thiele were at the Village Vanguard in Greenwich Village in November of 1961, a legendary place where jazz giants often clustered about like moths around a yellow light. Now the John Coltrane quartet and Impulse were there to document the evening on *Live At The Village Vanguard*. They were captured as "live" as any jazz music has ever been captured by the engineering genius of Van Gelder.

In the early sixties, evening television news reported an expanding war in exotic, tropical Vietnam. Often the camera jerked as sharp bursts of automatic rifle fire rattled out. In many respects, the Impulse group was the musical version of television's documentary war correspondents. For, like television's war correspondents, they were on a front line of battle, intent on bringing the event to a listening audience, changing the event as little as possible in the process of recording. It was one of those rare times when the philosophy of a business enterprise and an artist were in synchronization, leading each side to support the other. It was an eloquent and fitting summons to the members of the Coltrane group.

The listener is fortunate to hear the famous group coalesce on the first three of the more than thirty Impulse albums Coltrane would record. These albums were *Africa/Brass* in May and June of 1961 and *Live At The Village Vanguard* and *Impressions* in November of 1961. These dates mark a new direction for Coltrane, a direction away from many of his Atlantic-label faithful and into some truly unexplored territory. As such they denote a change from his previous structured compositions to new, loosely free and spontaneous musical ramblings.

The right record company at the right time. An amazing jazz producer who always kept the faith. A recording genius. A group of superb musicians led by a master musician. The daily ideas which swirled through Coltrane's mind: the music of India, of the Middle East, of Africa. His new conception of rhythm and a meticulous exploration of the particular moment in time.

All of these came together during the latter part of 1961 and helped launch Coltrane on his musical voyage.

Anarchists

A final ingredient in the initial Coltrane group was Eric Dolphy, one of Coltrane's closest friends. As a friend recalls, "John always told me that outside of Sonny Rollins, Eric Dolphy was his only true friend." This interesting quotation helps explain the phenomenal burst of creative energy the group experienced during the short nine months Dolphy was with them.

Few jazz critics ever consider Dolphy a member of the classic Coltrane group of the sixties. He joined them in the summer of 1961 during their first major tour and was out of the group, thanks largely to vicious criticism, by the spring of 1962.

Yet despite the shortness of his stay in the group and the criticism he received, Dolphy, with Coltrane himself, was the major architect of an incredible number of both live and studio albums from this period. The live music can be heard on *Live At The Village Vanguard* and *Impressions*, and the studio music on *Olé Coltrane* and *Africa/Brass*. The brilliant compositional work of Dolphy is especially apparent on *Africa/Brass*, for which he wrote the orchestration. On *Olé Coltrane*, recorded two weeks before *Africa/Brass*, the high-register flute and alto sax work of Dolphy helps push the emerging Coltrane group into unique musical spaces. A little more than six months later, at the end of November 1961, Dolphy made his last recording with the group during a live concert in Copenhagen. The album was never distributed in the United States because it was a bootleg work.

But even more than representing a particular period in the Coltrane music of the sixties, Dolphy set the tone, the energy level, for much of the amazing music soon to follow. In some respects he was an Elvin Jones of the horn as he kept pushing Coltrane higher and higher during those extended solo flights so common to this period. Dolphy was the master of the bass clarinet. Never before had anyone pulled such a bone-chilling low-register roar out of the horn, which had rarely been used in a jazz context. The great Jimmy Giuffre played it during the early part of his career almost exclusively in the low register; as Giuffre often pointed out, he did this because he was unable to do anything else. By the second half of the fifties Giuffre moved from the low to the high register of the instrument as his proficiency increased.

Giuffre's change was only partly a result of his increased technical abilities on the clarinet. In a large sense it was also an attempt to find a secure place for the instrument after the Europeanized "cool jazz" sound of groups such as The Modern Jazz Quartet and Dave Brubeck left little space for it in the new jazz. As critic Joachim Berendt notes, the clarinet was in a dilemma because it didn't seem to fit into the "saxophonized sound of modern jazz," its traditional tone clashing too much with the saxophone.

Eric Dolphy was the first to bring a totally new sound to the bass clarinet and, in the process, a unique new sound into all of jazz. His scorching, wildly emotional expression on the instrument combined with an immense visionary power gave listeners, as critic Berendt notes, "the feeling that he was not playing the traditional bass clarinet, which had always appeared somewhat old-fashioned, but rather a totally new instrument that had never been heard before." This Dolphy sound had many of the qualities Coltrane was looking for.

It was no coincidence that Dolphy arrived at a close approximation of the sounds Coltrane was after. The two had become friends around 1954, when Coltrane was playing with Johnny Hodges and Dolphy was working the Los Angeles studio scene and studying under the well-respected reedman Buddy Collette and the conservatory instructor Lloyd Reese. Both musicians were relative unknowns in the middle stage of apprenticeships to other well-known musicians. And both were attempting to carve out their own musical space in an art form which was increasingly intellectualizing itself as it moved away from the "hot" bebop style toward the "cool" modern jazz style. There was little room for the unique ideas of Dolphy and Coltrane in this evolving jazz and they found themselves alone in a strange twilight zone somewhere between hard bop and cool jazz.

They were greatly influenced by Charlie Parker, but neither wanted to simply perpetuate Parker's sound and style. Placed by circumstances beyond their control in a present they couldn't identify with, but bound to teachers in a past they couldn't escape from, they looked to the future for their salvation. In V.S. Naipaul's *A Bend In The River*, the novelist speaks about a village on the east coast of Africa where "People lived as they had always done (with) no break between past and present. All that had happened in the past was washed away; there was only the present. It was as though, as a result of some disturbance in the heavens, the early morning light was always receding into the darkness, and men lived in a perpetual dawn." During the early fifties, Coltrane and Dolphy were similar to the men of Naipaul's village.

For Coltrane, the "perpetual dawn" state at this time came from drugs as much as from conflicting musical directions. His friendship with Dolphy developed during that period when heroin and alcohol dominated his life. Coltrane needed change during this difficult period. He needed to discipline himself and to learn to control the incredible mood swings. He needed to set some goals in life and to decide how important music was to him. He needed to keep learning from the masters about him, from those who possessed more knowledge. And he needed to come to some kind of terms with all the drugs in his life and determine if drugs and music could coexist.

He needed many things at the time, but more than anything else he needed a strong friendship to show him there was a fellow traveler along the lonely path, that he wasn't cracking up. He needed to know there was another who saw some of the strange visions he saw in the strange "perpetual dawn" atmosphere. Eric Dolphy's friendship during this difficult period filled this important need and Dolphy became that fellow traveler. The two began talking music, discussing what was being done, and quickly found they had many similar ideas.

Dolphy was born in Los Angeles in 1928, and was only two years younger than Coltrane. In 1954, he lived with his parents in the Watts section of the city. Behind the house they built Eric a small studio. Working mainly as a studio sideman while attending Los Angeles City College, Dolphy was an aspiring but unknown freelance musician. His major break came a few years after he first met Coltrane, when he became a member of the Chico Hamilton Quintet.

The Hamilton Quintet helped launch Dolphy into prominence but did little to help answer some of the searching questions he was asking. Hamilton was a driving drummer, but his ideas were too imbued with the West Coast "cool" style for the emerging Dolphy style. A founding member of the Gerry Mulligan Quartet in 1953, he played a swinging jazz chamber music which was extremely common in West Coast jazz of the fifties.

The passionate playing of Dolphy within the "cool" confines of the Hamilton Quintet went too much against his grain and in 1960 he left Los Angeles and moved to New York to join Charles Mingus. In New York with Mingus, his eccentric ideas found sympathetic ears and within a short time he found himself one of the leaders of the new avant-gardists. By early 1961 Dolphy had left Mingus and recorded with such luminaries as Ornette

Coleman, Oliver Nelson and Gunther Schuller.

During this same time, the Coltrane group was coming together and playing various New York club dates. Dolphy asked his old friend if he could sit in on a few of their gigs and Coltrane said yes, of course he could. Dolphy sat in with the group and Coltrane felt this gave it an immediate boost. He related to Don DeMichael in the September 29, 1960, issue of *Down Beat* that Dolphy "...turned us all around. I'd felt at ease with just a quartet till then, but he came in and it was like having another member of the family. He'd found another way to express the same thing we had found one way to do." Coltrane talks about their relationship, noting that "We've been close for quite a while...We watched music. We always talked about it, discussed what was being done down through the years, because we love music."

When Dolphy joined the group many of the ideas from the Coltrane-Dolphy discussions were put into music. As Coltrane says, "We began to play some of the things we had only talked about before." One of the main things they had talked about over the years was the type of musical space which might exist between the notes in the Western musical system, the music of the European classical heritage. Dolphy was fascinated by the idea of so-called "quarter tones" which had long been a prime element of Western music. In certain ways, these tones approximated those spaces between the notes they were searching for.

Birds sing in quarter tones and Dolphy had always been interested in their unique sounds. As he tells

DeMichael in the above *Down Beat* interview, "At home I used to play, and the birds always used to whistle with me. I would stop what I was working on and play with the birds." Dolphy goes on to tell DeMichael how bird calls had been recorded and then slowed down in playback, and that they had a timbre similar to that of a flute. And when a symphony flutist recorded these bird calls and played the recording at fast speed it sounded like birds. "Birds have notes in between our notes," Dolphy says. "You try to imitate something they do and, like, maybe it's between F and F#, and you'll have to go up or come down on the pitch. It's really something! And so, when you get playing, this comes. You try to do some things on it. Indian music has something of the same quality—different scales and quarter tones. I don't know how you label it, but it's pretty."

The music Dolphy and Coltrane were creating, though, was not "pretty" to the critics. After his work on *Africa/ Brass* and *Olé Coltrane*, Dolphy joined the Coltrane quartet while they were on tour, and the famous quartet metamorphosed into a quintet. The interaction between the musicians seemed immediately supercharged with the addition of Dolphy and pushed Coltrane to new heights. But many jazz critics of the early sixties were afraid of the heights of the emerging new free jazz movement. And much of this new music was being created by the new Coltrane Quintet on tour.

Dolphy joined them on the West Coast and John Tynan, the associate editor of *Down Beat*, caught their engagement at the Renaissance Club in Hollywood. In the November

23, 1961, *Down Beat* he wrote, "I listened to a horrifying demonstration of what appears to be a growing anti-jazz trend exemplified by these foremost proponents of what is termed avant-garde music. I heard a good rhythm section...go to waste behind nihilistic exercises of two horns...Coltrane and Dolphy seem intent on deliberately destroying swing." Tynan concludes, "They seem bent on pursuing an anarchistic course in their music that can only be termed anti-jazz."

The term "anti-jazz" was picked up by influential critic Leonard Feather and used as a basis for some scathing articles in *Show* and *Down Beat* magazines on the Coltrane quintet. The reaction from readers, as DeMichael later remarked in the April 12, 1962, issue of *Down Beat*, was "immediate, heated and about evenly divided." One of the recurring charges of the critics was that their music was too long. Don DeMichael notes in the April 12 *Down Beat* that "Coltrane and Dolphy play on and on, past inspiration and into monotony."

In his book *The Jazz Tradition*, one of the finest jazz histories ever written, critic Martin Williams offers some perceptive insights about this period of extended performances. "As he pursued modality...evenings with Coltrane, a vertical player working with minimal harmonic understructures, began to sound to some listeners like long vamps-til-ready, or furious, unattached cadenzas, or lengthy monotones introducing rhumbas or songs that never got played." Williams quotes a Coltrane fan at the time telling him that "I went to hear Coltrane last night. He played forty-five minutes of C-minor ninths." Williams adds that "forty-five minutes on a C-minor pedal tone, it became increasingly clear, does not lead to musical freedom." Williams concludes that "I know that Coltrane's audiences were usually enthralled. I know the sincerity, the powerful and authentic emotion, and the frequent skill involved...and yet...I was, and am, repeatedly disengaged. After three or four minutes, my attention wanders, and giving the records try after try does not seem to help."

Perhaps much of the criticism of the time would have been different if critics had spent more time in the clubs catching Coltrane live rather than listening to him on record. Whatever the case, critics such as Williams, Tynan and Feather correctly aired the concerns of many of the previous Coltrane faithful who felt their prophet from the late 1950s abandoned them in the early 1960s. The great compositional Coltrane of such beautifully structured pieces as "Giant Steps," "Countdown" and "Spiral" seemed nowhere to be found during this period. Where was the strongly melodic Coltrane who was able to make powerful statements in short musical spaces of four or five minutes? This Coltrane was now replaced by a man who would often ramble on during live performances for upwards of an hour.

The reaction built as listeners and critics jumped on a huge anti-Coltrane bandwagon. The rising negative reaction to the music forced Coltrane and Dolphy to offer some public response. They responded in the April 12, 1962, issue of *Down Beat* in an interview with Don DeMichael. In response to the question "What are John Coltrane and Eric Dolphy trying to do?" Dolphy answered, saying "What I'm trying to do I find enjoyable (and) inspiring...It helps me play, this feel. It's like you have no idea what you're going to do next. You have an idea, but there's always that spontaneous thing that happens. This feeling, to me, leads the whole group."

Coltrane was more philosophical in his response to DeMichael's question. "I think the main thing a musician would like to do is to give a picture to the listener of the many wonderful things he knows of and senses in the universe. That's what music is to me—it's just another way of saying this is a big, beautiful universe we live in, that's been given us, and here's an example of just how magnificent and encompassing it is. That's what I would like to do. I think that's one of the greatest things you can do in life, and we all try to do it in some way. The musician's way is through his music." He adds that music is "a reflection of the universe. Like having life in miniature."

• • •

For a number of years only the tracks "Spiritual," "Softly As In A Morning Sunrise," "Chasin' the Trane," "India" and "Impressions" were available from the famous 1961 Village Vanguard engagement. But in 1977, fifteen years after this high-energy period for Coltrane, Impulse added another record to the group with the release of an album titled *The Other Village Vanguard Tapes*. The entire album was made from previously unreleased tapes during those four momentous evenings at the Village Vanguard. The release of this important album more than doubles the available music from this period.

With the issuance of *The Other Village Vanguard Tapes*, six additional tracks are placed into this important body of live recordings. Other versions of "Chasin' the Trane" and "India" are added and there is a short reworking of "Greensleeves," which was first recorded on *Africa/Brass*. Importantly, the tapes contain three extended pieces, among the longest Coltrane would ever record. Two of these pieces are titled "Spiritual," and the other simply "Untitled Original." One of the "Spiritual" pieces is over twelve minutes long and the other is over twenty minutes long. "Untitled Original" is over eighteen minutes long. If one wants to hear the controversial Coltrane music of this period, the *Other Village Vanguard Tapes* album is the best place to start.

In the music from the Village Vanguard date the reasons for the division of the Coltrane faithful of the late fifties and early sixties quickly become obvious. A good example of the new Coltrane of long spontaneous improvisational solos is the piece "Chasin' the Trane" from the Vanguard date. It was named by recording engineer Rudy Van Gelder because of all the chasing around he had to do with his microphone at the Vanguard to keep it only a few inches from Coltrane and Dolphy. Critic Martin Williams sees it as the key Coltrane performance from this period, noting that Coltrane's improvising on it has become "more horizontal, more linear than previously." Still, Williams feels Coltrane's use of reiterated phrases seems "deliberately repetitive and incantive." He adds that one man's incantation "is another man's monotony."

If the piece "Chasin' the Trane" meanders in the new free jazz way, the composition "Impressions" borrows an opening line from Debussy and then punches out at the listener in one of the strongest jolts of musical electricity that Coltrane would ever record. In its reiteration of certain phrases, "Impressions" finds a vague similarity to "Chasin' the Trane," but unlike "Chasin' the Trane," where an increasingly horizontal Coltrane horn finds itself meandering at times, the powerful opening line of "Impressions" relentlessly pounds away at the listener like the surf of some great ocean. One note is stated, then restated in a three-note sequence. The three-note sequence is then restated in a nine-note sequence. Then the single note is returned to, but it is different and the three-and nine-note sequences adjust themselves accordingly to the new note. This 1-3-9 sequence becomes a constantly shifting tonal center around which the Dolphy-Coltrane solos are formed. With the continual repetition around these centers, the composition borrows heavily from the strong modal period of Miles Davis captured on *Kind Of Blue* in 1959, and especially the Davis composition "So What."

In this sense, "Impressions" stands alone from music of this period and its incantatory effect or chant-like repetition. While much of the Coltrane music from this time lulls the listener into it, "Impressions" immediately strikes out at the listener without any preliminaries. Whereas much of the controversial longer pieces of the period is extended exploration of Eastern scale systems, "Impressions" depends more on the unique sequential rhythm groups and the memorable melody it creates. In many ways the composition serves as a final rallying cry of the Coltrane group. After two years of experimentation to find the correct group and an appropriate sound, everything seems to come together on "Impressions."

It is almost as if Coltrane is purging himself from negative past feelings and the questioning and doubt which tormented him through much of the fifties. The message of "Impressions" is stated so forcefully and with such exquisite clarity of method and purpose that little room is left for any vestiges of self-doubt. After creating "Africa," "India," "Chasin' the Trane" and "Impressions" he could never return to that old territory of the fifties.

 *Spaceways*

The early sixties were a period of great experimentation for Coltrane in his search for his style and the proper combination of musicians and context to contain this style. Musical ideas from other cultures permeated much of the experimentation as he attempted to approximate the mysterious inner sounds he was hearing. More often than not the search was wide open, unrestricted by time limitations, so that he was able to pursue the ideas through new musical dimensions to places no one had ever been.

The two-year period is difficult to label because so many facets of Coltrane emerged during the experiments. There was the compositional Coltrane on *Africa/Brass* and *Coltrane Jazz*, and there was the spontaneous Coltrane on *Live At The Village Vanguard*. There was the spontaneous and compositional Coltrane on *Impressions*. There was the warm, reminiscent Coltrane on compositions such as "Untitled Original" off *Coltrane Legacy*. And there was the wildly free Coltrane on pieces such as "Chasin' the Trane" from the live Village Vanguard recordings.

The only definition for the period is one of great transition. One phase of his life was ending while another phase was still in embryonic form. Much like the people of V.S. Naipaul's novel, *A Bend in the River,* he lived these few years in a "perpetual dawn," unable to fully escape his past yet unable to see the new ideas in the clarity of the noonday sun. The musical creatures he often conjured up in these early morning hours, though, were often spectacular.

Not only was it a transition time for Coltrane, but it was also a transition time for all of jazz. The cool, European jazz of the late fifties offered an increasingly inadequate context to express some of the heated, emotional issues of the sixties. It was a subtle, subdued music which was becoming obsolete in a developing period of confrontation.

In this peculiar in-between time, some musicians refused to let the old memories die while others blasted away at the old structure with the same force and vehemence of Charlie Parker and Dizzy Gillespie fifteen years earlier. It was one of those crucial times in art when past traditions and techniques prove impossible to work with and when some form of new synthesis seemed called for.

As it was in the forties, two main schools of jazz stood in direct conflict—the school representing the ordered past of the music, stressing the compositional elements, the "Ellington jazz," and the school of young modernists who placed more importance on the spontaneous, chaotic and stream-of-consciousness present. Somewhere between the two was Coltrane. For those two great forces in jazz and life, order and chaos, now waged their greatest battle not only outwardly between various schools of musicians but inside the spirit of John Coltrane. The explosions from the inner fusion of these two elements is often spectacular in the music of this period. But at other times the fusion doesn't happen and the listener is aware of the torture Coltrane was going through to exorcise the spirits which possessed him. However, the individual successes and the failures are not as important as that, for the first time in jazz, the forces of order and chaos were now doing battle under one roof, inside the music of one man.

The transitional period was not the exclusive province of John Coltrane or jazz. America was also going through a major transitional period. Slowly, an entire age in American history was ending and a new one beginning.

• • •

The transitional state was expressed in the new, emerging music of free jazz. It was a subtle emergence, though, not possessed with the volcanic force of the bebop school. Those conducting experiments in the new music worked, for the most part, alone, often in their own homes. There never was a central club for the new music, like Minton's had been for the bebop movement. There existed no grand central bands such as Billy Eckstine's of the forties in which new ideas could be shared.

In *The Making of Jazz* James Lincoln Collier notes that Cecil Taylor was in Boston "hammering away at a spavined piano in a ruined practice studio littered with broken glass," while Ornette Coleman was practicing in a Los Angeles garage and Steve Lacy, Roswell Rudd and

Herbie Nichols were playing in Dixieland bands for their living. It was the first true underground movement in the history of jazz and its small handful of practitioners found little acceptance initially in the jazz community.

Certain events in the emerging music stood out from its overall subtlety. One of these events took place in 1957 when Ornette Coleman formed his first quartet with trumpeter Don Cherry in Los Angeles. In the same year pianist Cecil Taylor appeared at the Newport Jazz Festival. And in 1959 and 1960 the Coleman Quartet with Don Cherry, Charlie Haden, and Billy Higgins successfully appeared at the Five Spot.

Coltrane himself was treated to a large dose of the new ideas in his joint effort with Don Cherry on the album *The Avant-Garde*. In 1960 the influential Coleman statement of the new free jazz form was made on the album *Free Jazz*. It was a bold experiment using a double quartet of two trumpets, two reeds, two basses and two drummers in a spontaneous, collective improvisation that lasted over thirty-six minutes.

For those who followed the developing free jazz movement, the 1960 Coleman album was not a total surprise. A little earlier, he had hinted at many of these ideas on his album *The Shape of Jazz to Come*. However, on *Free Jazz* the earlier ideas find a powerful expression and make it difficult for the jazz community to continue to ignore the angry young underground musicians.

Martin Williams in *The Jazz Tradition* sees the album as "a flawed and brilliant work" which is possessed with a "turbulent, purposeful, harrowing, and joyous texture." Interestingly enough, Eric Dolphy is present. Soon after his work on it he would join Coltrane. "Jazz is a music full of the stuff of life," Williams notes, and concludes that *"Free Jazz* has the stuff of life in it as no other recorded performance I know of."

The two Coleman albums, *The Shape of Jazz to Come* and *Free Jazz,* provide a rallying point, a Minton's on record, for the new free jazz musicians. The albums did not give any definitive statements, for the turbulent times didn't allow for this. They simply suggested new escape routes from the intellectual, European cool jazz stalemate of the late fifties, providing musicians with new techniques and methods more than finished musical statements. The music of Coleman gave them tools to make their own explorations rather than imposing any structure of playing form onto them.

On the pieces from *The Shape of Jazz,* Martin Williams observes that "An idea appears, inspired perhaps by a single note or accent. It is phrased and rephrased, offered from every conceivable angle, developed sequentially until it yields another idea...Or it appears and reappears periodically in various guises...as a kind of point of reference. Patterns of tension and release are thus set up by the introduction and ultimate development of brief motives, or by their appearance and reappearance."

This daring new technique forces a reassessment of previous jazz foundations. The music always had its revolutionaries, such as Jelly Roll Morton, Louis Armstrong,

Bix Beiderbecke, Coleman Hawkins, Lester Young, Duke Ellington, Charlie Parker, Miles Davis and Thelonious Monk. All of them changed the music significantly, but for the most part they all worked within the system, never challenging the basic tenets of the whole structure. Their innovations were often spectacular and unique, but the questions they asked and the answers they provided centered mainly on variations of time signatures and new ways of stating the melody and harmony. They never seriously questioned the necessity for having these elements within the music.

As Martin Williams notes, the free jazz of the Coleman group did not "offer a further subdivision of the beat, as Armstrong, Lester Young, and Parker had done, but a greater variety and freedom in rhythm and phrases." Musical structure itself, rather than elements of the structure, was called into question by the new free jazz.

One of the major parts of jazz structure called into question was the theme-and-variations approach. The theme was stated at the beginning of the piece, variations on it were introduced and then resolved, until the initial theme was restated at the end. It had an ordered chronology, a beginning, middle and end. This chronological structure had not been questioned. No matter how unique and bold jazz ideas had been, they were always stated within this broad linear framework. It was a structure that previously could accommodate even the radical extremes of the music.

On Coleman's *The Shape of Jazz to Come* the old chronology was challenged. As Williams notes "it reassesses the theme-and-variations form for jazz" and "ultimately rejects the form...with good reason. For in a theme-and-variations approach the theme is primary and the variations secondary. But in jazz, the improvised variations are often the substance of the music." He remarks that an opening theme "may set a mood, fragments of melody, an area of pitch, or rhythmic patterns as points of departure for the players to explore. It need not set up patterns of chords or patterns of phrasing...if it does, these may be expanded, condensed and used freely." He was talking about one particular album but he might well have been talking about much of the new jazz.

Ornette Coleman was closest to the core of the new music, but a number of others were not too far away, borrowing and expanding on the Coleman ideas while at the same time contributing their own unique ideas. A list of these key players in the new music would have to include Cecil Taylor, Archie Shepp, Don Cherry, Albert Ayler, Rashsaan Roland Kirk and, the outer space cowboy himself, Sun Ra and his famous Sun Ra Arkestra. Like the music of Coleman, their ideas possessed a new freedom, a breakthrough, as Joachim Berendt notes, into the free space of atonality, as well as a new rhythmic conception characterized by the disintegration of meter, beat and symmetry.

The resulting music contained a mishmash of new ideas jumbled about in free-form statements. It was seldom melodic. For the most part any recognizable melodies were merely coincidental, with the coincidence lasting only a few seconds. It was a harsh, strident music, almost a direct antithesis of the understated cool jazz which preceded it. Often it sounded like a Dixieland band gone haywire or a Salvation Army band on LSD. The result was that the listener seldom had any musical "hook" to hang onto for his bearings. Always a controversial form, it was not music which received high radio airplay and developed legions of faithful followers. Even at the height of its popularity it was still supported by a relatively small number of hard-core believers.

The communication theorist Marshall McLuhan observed in *Understanding Media* "the medium is the message," meaning the context of communication is more important than the contents of communication. This was true with free jazz, where creative context seemed more the point than the final contents of this context. It was an effort to create a new medium of expression more than to create new contents within the medium.

Coltrane was listening with extreme interest to a number of the free jazz musicians like Pharoah Sanders, Archie Shepp and Albert Ayler during this time. In the book *Black Nationalism and the Revolution In Music*, he tells author Frank Kofsky that he had listened closely to Albert Ayler and that "He's something else (and) seems to be moving music into higher frequencies." On July 21, 1967, the Albert Ayler Quartet would play the invocation at Trane's funeral. Archie Shepp became the angry young intellectual of the free jazz movement. As LeRoi Jones once said about him, "Shepp is one of the most committed of jazz musicians, old or young, critically aware of the social responsibility of the black artist…In this sense, ethics and esthetics are one." It was through Coltrane's direct efforts that Shepp was able to record his first album with Impulse in 1964 and, in honor of Coltrane, Shepp named the album *Four For Trane*.

But the young free jazz musician who would later have the greatest impact on Coltrane's music was Pharoah Sanders. In the young Sanders Coltrane found an incredible spiritual strength. In certain ways he became the McCoy Tyner of the saxophone for Coltrane. However, unlike the Tyner of this period, Sanders' music was far from subtle. Jazz critic Brian Case comments that his first album *Pharoah Sanders* "showed a style that was composed entirely of extreme overblowing, screaming out clusters of notes, the line a furious supersonic scribbling." The wild and free sound of Sanders' sax served as a superb foil to Coltrane's frequent heaviness.

• • •

Like other important new free jazz musicians such as Julian Priester, Marion Brown, Ed Blackwell, Richard Evans and John Gilmore, Pharoah Sanders had served an apprenticeship in the amazing band of Herman "Sonny" Blount, more commonly known as Sun Ra. If the soul of the new jazz centered on the ideas of Ornette Coleman, then its spirit hovered somewhere near Sun Ra.

Starting as an arranger for Fletcher Henderson in the late forties, Sun Ra (Ra is one of the Egyptian sun gods) steadily developed cosmic jazz centering on a unique philosophical perspective on life. His preoccupation with exotic instruments like gongs, Moog synthesizers, massed timpani and rocksichord produced a strange otherworldly sound. In Sun Ra's music wind swooshes, bells jingle, and it quickly becomes evident that his music offers an astoundingly original vision. Much of it would have been the perfect background music for the popular television shows of this period such as "Twilight Zone" or "The Outer Limits."

On stage Sun Ra's musicians looked like space visitors dressed in their flowing robes, bright print shirts, bells, beads and light-up hats. Sun Ra himself usually wore a glittering metal skullcap he called his Sun Helmut. And often in the background, reinforcing Sun Ra's far-out image, were dancers, back-projected film and even fire-eaters. He called his group the Arkestra and their theme was "We Travel The Spaceways."

And travel them they did. A new plateau was reached in the music of Sun Ra, far out in space as Sun Ra would surely put it. More than provide new techniques to jazz musicians like Ornette Coleman, Sun Ra provided a broad new perspective for them, its dimensions only defined by the outer reaches of his expanding musical cosmos.

Sun Ra's unique universe was spiritual in nature, and this spirituality became a powerful force in the lives of the many important musicians always passing through the ranks of the famous Arkestra. It was as if Sun Ra was possessed with some mystical force which redirected the energy of those around him toward higher concerns.

The musicians of the Coleman school seemed to strike out at the world during this intense period, snapping at events and lingering beliefs of the old America like angry dogs. But Sun Ra and his Arkestra simply flew over the whole immediate mess of world and domestic affairs, a type of musical spaceship high above the emotionalism of everyday life on planet Earth. It wasn't that Sun Ra was out of touch with the civil rights movement and the developing war in Vietnam. He was never out of touch with any important earthly vibrations. Rather, he seemed to also be in touch with distant vibrations, and it was from these that he patterned his life and his music.

Albums such as *Angels & Demons At Play*, *Astro Black*, *Magic City* and *The Nubians Of Plutonia*, recorded in the sixties on his own Saturn label (reissued by Impulse) demonstrate his unique compositional abilities and an uncanny ability to summon forth powerful, provocative musical images. The albums were hand-painted and distributed by Arkestra members dressed in their space robes.

This was not the case with musicians of the Coleman free jazz group, who were more intent on destroying images in their stream-of-consciousness technique than in creating them. Unlike much of the dark music they created, Sun Ra's music was positive and often possessed a cheerful playfulness. For instance, the piece "Moonship Journey" from *Cosmos* sounds like a space version of the early rock tune "Sugar Shack." There is always an openness and approachability about Sun Ra's music and a warmth of feeling within it. Again, these were not qualities of the Coleman people. It was as if Sun Ra had arrived at a certain place in life while the others attempted to destroy the place they were in.

The 1977 Sun Ra album *Cosmos* on the Inner City label in many ways represents a certain fruition of Sun Ra's ideas about space he held during the sixties. Compositions address themselves to cosmic themes such as "Interstellar Low-Ways," "Journey Among The Stars" and "Jazz From An Unknown Planet." The music is evocative, inviting, promising new adventures for the listener who will stay with Sun Ra for the ride.

In retrospect, Sun Ra's genius and vision seem even greater because the cosmic thrust he injected into jazz, the spiritual perspective he has always blatantly preached in his music, the master jazz musicians who apprenticed with him, are what constitute the strongest force in jazz today, a force which comes from the spirit more than any other area.

Like an individual life, the history of jazz had progressed from the emotional music of Louis Armstrong and the early Dixieland bands to the intellectualized cool jazz of Dave Brubeck and Miles Davis. It had been at first a music for the body and soul, and then a music for the mind. Sun Ra was the embodiment of a growing number of important and dedicated musicians who felt that it was now the appropriate time for jazz to become the music of the spirit. For years the music had been moving toward this perspective, but the undercurrents of the movement were often difficult to see because it was such an all-pervasive movement.

Traditional changes in an art form, those of technique, style and method, are essentially internal because they change the content of the art form. Communication methods are refined and various schools stand in opposition to one another. Somehow and somewhere there is a certain logic to the whole thing. Influences are fairly traceable and, if one wants to spend a lot of time on the matter, a type of huge "family tree" can be brought forth.

On the other hand, nontraditional changes work at the medium itself rather than the contents of the medium and are more difficult to see. Everyone involved with the art form feels the new perspective to a certain extent, and it pervades everything like a fine mist, rolling in over the art form, impossible to totally escape but at the same time difficult to see.

This was the case with the growing spiritual perspective of jazz centered in Philadelphia in the forties. These years saw many conversions to the Islamic religion aided by musicians such as Ahmad Jamal and Art Blakey who brought Moslem teachers to America. Coltrane was living there and becoming friends with Moslems Yusef Lateef and McCoy Tyner, known as Sulieman Saud by friends. He was extremely moved by the Islamic religion and in fact married a Moslem woman.

Sun Ra was not a convert to the Islamic religion, but his music evidenced a sense of strength and conviction, important traits of Islam. In Sun Ra the new spiritual mist hanging over the jazz world finally coalesced within an individual musician. He had originally worked in Chicago, and moved to New York in 1960. Significantly, Coltrane had been familiar with Sun Ra's music in Chicago and often attended the Monday night sessions at Birdland when the Arkestra was playing in New York. Arkestra member John Gilmore recalls that Coltrane finally started visiting the Arkestra's studio on West 82nd Street, where Sun Ra gave him literature on outer space and where Gilmore showed Coltrane how to reach certain notes in the overtone series. Coltrane once said, "I listened to John Gilmore kind of closely before I made 'Chasin' the Trane'...So some of those things on there are really direct influences of listening to this cat, you see."

As Gilmore remembers, "Trane really wanted to play more avant-garde music, but he didn't get the foundation until he listened to Sun Ra a lot. I think we helped him get his Oriental and African music together, too. I'll tell you this, whenever I saw him after he'd studied with Sun Ra, he was smoking!"

Reflection

*S*un Ra's avant-garde ideas and the free jazz movement may have occupied a high priority in Coltrane's mind during the early sixties, but there is little musical evidence of this concern in his recorded music of 1962 and 1963. More than anything, Sun Ra's ideas were in a state of fermentation, ready to bear musical fruit at some later date.

It was an unusual time for Coltrane, a period of relative calm after the storm of the Village Vanguard period and the *Africa/Brass* session in 1961. It was a time when the searing flame and the burning immediacy of his message was reduced to a low pilot light. The period is seen by most critics as a musical backwater of his career and termed the "ballad years."

There were few original compositions, most of the music being a "Coltranized" repackaging of some traditional jazz standards such as "In A Sentimental Mood," "My One And Only Love" and "They Say It's Wonderful." Of the thirty-six pieces recorded by Coltrane between April 1962 and October 1963, only eight are original, a small number compared to the *Giant Steps* period from May 1959 to the end of December in 1961, which saw thirty-nine original compositions out of a total of sixty-five. In the earlier period, nearly two-thirds of the material is original, while in the latter period, less than one-fourth of the material is original. In contrast, Coltrane's highly creative period from November 1963 until his death in 1967 contained an amazing fifty-six original pieces from a total of sixty-two.

The contrast is also apparent in the number of albums. The earlier period, beginning with *Giant Steps* and continuing through the Village Vanguard material in late 1961, contains fifteen albums, while the late period, beginning in October 1963 and ending in March 1967, contains twenty albums. Separating these two periods of frenzied recording activity, somewhat like a peaceful lake between two great mountain ranges, is the "ballad period" and its cache of only five albums

Albums such as *Ballads* and *John Coltrane With Johnny Hartman* evidence a definite slowing down for Coltrane and an outwardly apparent turn away from the turbulent new free jazz. In some respects, it is a romantic and sentimental part of his life, an introspective time very similar to the time around *Kind of Blue* in the spring of 1959. *Duke Ellington And John Coltrane*, for instance, demonstrates a certain willingness on his part to return to some of the ideas of the great master of traditional, composed jazz. The piece "Big Nick" from the Ellington album finds Duke Ellington replacing McCoy Tyner on piano. It begins with the kind of soft-paced melody one might hear in the background of a *Little Rascals* film, with Coltrane slowly walking through the music with his horn. About a minute into the piece he cuts loose an improvisational barrage of notes while Duke continues stating the pleasantly simple melody.

Tyner would have pushed it more, but with Ellington everything seems anchored, including Coltrane, who builds his music around, and not above, the Duke. It's a far cry from the wildly spontaneous music of "Chasin' the Trane" or the heavily sober ideas of "Spiritual" from the live Village Vanguard date. It seems light years away from the strong compositional abilities demonstrated in *Giant Steps* and *Africa/Brass*.

This calm and peaceful flatness between the two mighty mountain ranges of creativity in the geography of his life leads one to search out the reason for the peace in the midst of a raging musical storm. Speculation on the matter still abounds in the jazz community, and the commonly accepted notion is that the ballad period was primarily created by external pressures on Coltrane to ease the growing alienation many Coltrane faithful were feeling toward the extended solos and Eastern-influenced music he was creating with Eric Dolphy. Interestingly enough, a few months after the famous *Down Beat* interview in which he and Dolphy responded to critics, Impulse issued the *Ballads* album which marked the beginning of the so-called "ballad years."

Despite external pressures pushing Coltrane and Impulse toward a more commercial music, internal pressures also strongly influenced the decision to slow his pace. In *John Coltrane*, Bill Cole notes that he was having problems with his reeds and mouthpiece as early as the fall of 1961 and quotes him saying "I got dissatisfied with my mouthpiece and I had some work done on this thing, and instead of making it better, it ruined it. It really discouraged me a little bit, because there were certain aspects of playing—that certain fast thing that I was reaching for—that I couldn't get because I had damaged this thing, so I just had to curtail it...But after a year or so it passed."

A little later, from April to October of 1963, Elvin Jones again returned to prison on another drug charge. During his absence, he was replaced by Roy Haynes, heard backing up the quartet during their appearance at the 1963 Newport Jazz Festival. As great as Haynes was, he couldn't energize the group like Elvin. In October of 1963, Elvin returned to the group and his return is captured on *Live At Birdland*. Interestingly enough, the *Birdland* album marked the end of the ballad period and the beginning of a new period for Coltrane.

In the background during these years, but permeating his personal life, was the breakup of his marriage to Naima. It is difficult to say where the problems started, but it is clear by May of 1960 he was seeing another woman. She was a tall, slim, white woman who had moved to New York in the late fifties to be close to musicians. Through Sonny Rollins she was introduced to Coltrane.

She kept a diary during her relationship with him and recorded her their first meeting on May 21, 1960, writing:

"I got up early and went to Brooklyn to learn how to make sweet potato pie from Mama Gracie. Went to the Jazz Gallery and spoke to John after the first set."

"I've brought you a present," she told him.

"You?" he asked her.

"Me," she told him.

"He tasted the pie I'd baked for him," she writes in the diary, "and licked his fingers."

"Let's talk sometime," he told her.

Sweet potato pie had for years been his passion. A few weeks later, on June 8, 1960, she met him again and records the meeting in her diary:

"John called at 2:15 a.m. and wanted to see me. He picked me up at 4:30 a.m., took me to a Harlem hotel. He was more than considerate with me, knowing of my inexperience, and initiated me into his ways of extreme tenderness. It took me less than a week to fall in love with him...And it all started right after I had taken him the sweet potato pie."

Their relationship continued for over three years until a new woman came into his life. Her name was Alice McLeod and she was a jazz pianist. In the summer of 1963, Coltrane left Naima and began living with Alice. As she recalls, "We were both traveling in a particular spiritual direction, John and myself, so it seemed only natural for us to join forces. It was like God uniting two souls together. I think John could have just as easily married another woman, though. Not myself and not because I was a musician, but any woman who had the particular attributes or qualities to help him fulfill his life mission as God wanted him to."

Born in Detroit in 1937, Alice was a shy, introspective woman who had started her musical career playing school dances at Cass Technical High School. Graduating from Cass in 1955, she played a number of dates around Detroit for a few years. In 1959 she left the country and went to Paris to study with the legendary Bud Powell. When she returned to Detroit in the fall of 1960, she met Coltrane at a party. After discovering that she was a musician he asked her to "Tell me more." As Alice recalls, "From the way he looked at me, I knew we would be meeting again."

And they did meet again a few months later, during the early part of 1961 when Coltrane was playing with Miles Davis at the Olympia Theater in Paris. She recalls that "I felt I was receiving a message from John through his music, as if he was talking to me personally."

The next time they met was over two years later at the Birdland club in July of 1963, when they were both playing on the same bill. Alice was with vibraphonist Terry Gibbs' quartet, and part of the band's routine was for Alice to play vibraphones. Since she had studied the vibraphone her playing was quite impressive, and during intermission Coltrane sought her out and admiringly said to her, "I never knew you could play vibes," to which she replied, "You never knew a lot of things about me." Looking into her eyes, he said, "Well, I'm going to make it my business to find out all I can about you." Shortly after the Birdland date they began living together, and were married in 1966.

• • •

In the debate over the reasons behind Coltrane's peculiar "ballad years" one can find support for both theories of internal or external pressures. But another explanation goes beyond the contemporary events of his life and places the "ballad years" in a larger context. In this context these years do not seem strange and unique but rather a reoccurrence of a lifelong pattern started during his early years in Philadelphia when he moved between extremes of hyperactivity and quiet reflection.

At first these periods of reflection seemed imposed on Coltrane from without; the result of losing positions in bands, largely due to his problem with drugs. Losing jobs took him off the high-energy life of touring with bands and returned him to Philadelphia. This happened when he lost his job with the Jimmy Heath band in 1948, with the Gillespie band in 1951, and with the Hodges band in 1953. He found himself playing at places like Joe Pitt's Musical Bar, or the Zanzibar, or backing unknowns like Shirley Scott and Bill Carney.

But in retrospect, searching for the cause of these periods seems less important than investigating what transpired within them. Many of Coltrane's contemporaries became lost in narcotic fogs during periods of unemployment and disgrace. However, Coltrane began using them to gain a broad-ranging education in music and philosophy. His creative use of these periods led him to his enrollment at the Granoff School of Music and the resulting exposure to classical composers such as Bartok and Stravinsky. And it also led him to readings and study of the teachings of world-famous philosophers representing different religions.

He came to view these "rest stops" along life's rushing superhighway as both welcome and nourishing periods. He came to realize that they were basic parts of an inner man who was essentially a shy and reserved person placed in the public spotlight more by the adulation of others than by an internal drive to be there. In many ways he was a quiet philosopher who also happened to be a visionary artist. The quiet philosopher was always as important to Coltrane as the wildly searching musician, and he worked to bring both of them into some type of peaceful coexistence.

After the mid-1950s, when he recognized the quiet periods were necessary, he almost began to search them out. They offered small oases in the often hot and barren desert of exploration as he pushed toward distant musical mountain peaks of increasing intensity. One of these reflective times centered around the spring of 1957, when he stayed in his room for two weeks to battle heroin addiction. Another period was the quiet reflective period in the late fifties with Miles Davis, captured on pieces like "All Blues" from *Kind Of Blue*, a period similar to his ballad years. Another was in 1960, a year filled with a number of Atlantic label reissues.

The extreme swing between peaks of musical creativity and valleys of rest and reflection became a recurring pattern. Periods of rest followed or preceded periods of intense growth, exploration and creativity. For after the low and quiet periods, the pursuit of the vision began again in earnest. After the low point of losing his job with

Dizzy Gillespie, he grew tremendously from 1952 to 1954 under the tutelage of master musicians Earl Bostic and Johnny Hodges. Again, in the mid-1950s, after walking the bar and playing with acts like Daisy Mae and the Hepcats, he joined Miles Davis. And in 1957, after experiencing another deep valley in his life, he went forward into the legendary date at the Five Spot with Thelonious Monk. After the reflectiveness on *Kind Of Blue*, he created *Giant Steps* in an effort of gushing creativity. And after the peacefulness of 1960 and the Atlantic reissues, he quickly journeyed back into the controversial core of the jazz world.

The ballad years were another one of the rest stops along the great Coltrane highway of musical exploration. But this time it would be the final rest stop right before his most momentous musical journey. Immediately following the quiet ballad years stood the years 1964, 1965 and 1966 and the highest musical peaks he would ever attempt to surmount. In these final years there would be little rest and reflection for Coltrane as he moved forward to create what many believe is his most important work.

As Bob Dylan sang, "The times, they are a changing." They certainly were in 1962 and 1963, when Dylan was rising in popularity. The bumper car of American history was spinning more erratically now, knocking over the beliefs of the dying age like a drunk in a china shop. Everyone seemed confused, everything seemed disoriented. Perhaps the little old man behind the curtain who turned out to be the Wizard of Oz really was running the whole show.

While frightened young teenagers were sent off to a

war in tropical jungles, others put the matter out of their minds at the Peppermint Lounge in New York "twisting" the night away to the music of Joey Dee and the Starlighters. The Honeycombs asked "Have I The Right?" and Del Shannon wondered about his little "Runaway." In the midst of twisting about on dance floors, pregnant women who had been prescribed a sedative known as thalidomide began delivering deformed babies, some with flippers instead of limbs.

In this strange period of American history the civil rights movement was growing and a great confrontation was at hand. In January of 1963, Governor George Wallace of Alabama said "I draw the line in the dust and toss the gauntlet before the feet of tyranny, and I say segregation now, segregation tomorrow, segregation forever." In May of 1963, after a large civil rights demonstration in Birmingham, Alabama, the city reluctantly agreed to the desegregation of public facilities after the twin bombings of homes of black leaders, resulting in the calling of state troopers. On August 28, 1963, over 200,000 civil rights demonstrators gathered in Washington, D.C., for the largest civil rights demonstration in history.

The growing civil rights movement reached a terrible peak in September. On Sunday morning, September 15, 1963, a dozen sticks of dynamite were planted in the basement of the 16th Street Baptist Church in Birmingham, Alabama. At 10:25 a.m. an explosion blew several man-sized holes in the church walls, injuring fourteen parishioners and killing four black girls age eleven through fourteen. The little girls had just finished their Sunday school lesson called "The Love That Forgives."

Trane heard the news that afternoon on the radio. He felt strongly that a personal statement from him was called for. No longer could he keep himself out of the craziness of the times, no longer could he continue playing ballads while children were being killed. This particular rest period was now over.

In October and November of 1963, the Coltrane Quartet was booked into New York's Birdland, and on October 8th Impulse recorded *Coltrane Live At Birdland*, the first live date they had done since the Vanguard period in November of 1961. Apart from being the first live date in almost two years for Trane, *Coltrane Live At Birdland* also marks his return to composed, original material. A unifying theme is Coltrane's feeling of deep frustration and anger over the racial violence and a heavy sorrow, at times bordering almost on despair, brought on by an increasingly divided country. As Cecil Taylor observed, "Coltrane has a feeling for the hysteria of the times," and this feeling is superbly communicated on the *Birdland* album.

The hysteria centered on the black man's plight in the America of the early sixties. It was the first time Trane had specifically directed his energies to this plight. Earlier works such as *Giant Steps*, *Coltrane Jazz*, *Africa/Brass* and *Live At The Village Vanguard* certainly expressed a concern for the struggle for racial equality, but the concern permeated the atmosphere like nightclub smoke. In this sense, it seemed to be something which Trane had not yet directly approached. *Giant Steps* and *Coltrane Jazz* present unique harmonic discoveries and tributes to those closest to him in life while *Africa/Brass* evidences a desire to move jazz toward an African and Eastern direction. The Vanguard recording finds Trane exploring extended improvisation in the long piece "Spiritual." While all evidence a growing interest in his African heritage, they do not directly address themselves to the plight of blacks in the America of the middle sixties.

But *Coltrane Live At Birdland* indicates an overriding concern with the current critical racial situation. Of the five pieces on the *Birdland* album, two stand out in strong relief because of the power and expression Trane summons to translate this crazy, weird period into music. One of the pieces, his tribute to the slain black children in the Birmingham church, "Alabama," is one of the darkest, most melancholy pieces he would ever play. In an effort to give it the feeling of whispered prayer, he dives deep into the low register of his horn, an area he seldom explored. In an effort to give the music a strong sense of urgency, the composition's overall structure is built around a memorial speech the Reverend Martin Luther King delivered for the slain children. After reading the text of the speech on an airplane, Coltrane wrote "Alabama" using the speech's rhythmic inflections.

Juxtaposed against the heavy-handed melancholy of "Alabama" on *Coltrane Live At Birdland* is the positive, forward-looking composition "The Promise." Whereas "Alabama" shows resignation about the dark current state,

"The Promise" goes beyond this resignation, finding inspiration and light in the future. One composition states the feelings of the time while the other attempts to lead the listener forward into a new peaceful world away from the current turmoil.

A few minutes into "The Promise" McCoy Tyner explodes with a strong extended solo evidencing a new direction. He moves from providing a base for the group toward a new prominence in the quartet. The composition is energetic, displaying his musical ideas. After Coltrane's death, "The Promise" would become one of Tyner's favorites, constantly reworked during his career. One of the finest reworkings is captured by Milestone Records on the 1972 Tyner album of piano solos, *Echoes Of A Friend*, a tribute to Coltrane.

During the months following the Birdland date, the fiery temper of the times cooled and some major advances occurred in civil rights. In January of 1964, the Twenty-fourth Amendment to the U.S. Constitution took effect. The essential part of the new amendment was the prohibition of poll taxes in federal elections, widely used throughout the South to keep blacks from voting. In July of 1964, the Civil Rights Act was approved by Congress and signed by President Johnson. The Act outlawed racial discrimination in public places, employment, unions and federally aided programs. And in October of 1964, the Reverend Martin Luther King won the Nobel Peace Prize.

This relatively peaceful period is captured by Coltrane in April and June of 1964 on his next album after the

Birdland date. *Crescent* contains five original compositions, and features a more reflective and conservative Coltrane. Great effort is evidenced by the eight takes recorded before Trane was finally satisfied with the title cut.

The title cut has been appropriately described by C.O. Simpkins as a "majestic composition with great measured sweeps of sound" which has "the swaying sadness of a spiritual, and the grandness of an anthem." Critic Martin Williams writes about "Crescent" in *The Jazz Tradition*, noting that the "harsh dangers and exotic beauties" of Coltrane's musical travels are related on it through a horn which seems "natural" and possessed with "firmly established techniques." Elvin Jones seems to be the inspiration for "The Drum Thing." To C.O. Simpkins the piece gives the feeling of a "mysterious rain forest in which a horn chants its solemn meditation." A beautiful reflective quality is heard on "Lonnie's Lament," while "Bessie's Blues," dedicated to Bessie Smith, has an air of celebration. The "Wise One" was written as a tribute to the wisdom of Naima and its effect on Coltrane. It was a thank-you note to her for helping him make it through the rough terrain they had traveled through since their marriage in 1955. It was also a reminder that now, when a new woman was in his life, the soft, gentle ways of Naima were not forgotten.

Crescent offers a brief respite after the fire of *Coltrane Live At Birdland*. But any sense of peace would quickly disappear within weeks after *Crescent* was recorded. On June 29, 1964, Eric Dolphy died in Berlin, Germany, of complications resulting from coronary problems. Coltrane lost his best friend. It greatly affected Trane and the music he created throughout the rest of his life.

Dolphy's death had even wider implications of tragedy. It ended a life which was becoming tragic; his lack of critical acceptance had hastened his exit from the American jazz scene and his entry into the always accepting European jazz scene. A personal tragedy was developing when he died in Berlin.

But in the end, Dolphy's death was more than a personal tragedy; it hurt the entire jazz world. It can be compared to the early death of Clifford Brown in its impact on the music. More than anything else, Dolphy extended the range of jazz notes from the low humming of a bass clarinet to the shrill bird-like sound of a flute. The sound he achieved was often the most advanced in jazz.

Dolphy, though, was not much of a team player and this did not help his jazz career in America. However, his last album, the brilliant *Out To Lunch*, with such rising stars as Freddie Hubbard, Bobby Hutcherson, Richard Davis and Tony Williams, shows a move away from solo work toward group leadership. It was his first move in this new direction, and *Out To Lunch* promises that it would have been an interesting direction.

In the August 27, 1964, issue of *Down Beat* Trane expressed some of his sentiments for Eric Dolphy stating "Whatever I say would be an understatement. I can only say my life was made much better by knowing him. He was one of the greatest people I've ever known, as a man, a friend and a musician." As a final symbol of this wonderful friendship, Dolphy's parents presented Coltrane with their son's flute and bass clarinet. For the rest of his life Trane would cherish these two instruments, using them on a number of recording dates. He was carrying forth the voice of his friend.

Psalm

A silence of almost six months fell over Coltrane's horn, largely the result of Dolphy's death. Much was going on inside his head—new patterns and relationships were crystallizing like quartz, while some of the old mental furniture was shifted radically about. He seemed possessed with some new internal demon, eventually necessitating an exorcism.

The driving force is no longer directed outward at the injustice of the world like it was after the four black girls were killed and *Coltrane Live At Birdland*. The focus was now turned inward, as far inward as he has ever looked. It was a final period of reflection and regaining a perspective on life after the death of his closest friend.

The inward searching finally reached a land of great peacefulness and he saw the world in a new perspective. The path and goals were clear once again. A new sense of urgency and power took hold of his spirit and the baggage of the past fell away until he was once again that sole explorer on a historic trek through that great vast desert which opens before him like the Sahara. Everything took on a brilliant luminescence, that strange light which seems to come from inside objects as much as from outside. The light was radiant, a perpetual glow. As it was in 1957, he again feels touched by God.

On December 9, 1964, he took the quartet into the Impulse studios to record a statement of his feelings about God. The result was *A Love Supreme*. On the liner notes he said "This album is a humble offering to Him, an attempt to say 'Thank you, God' through our work, even as we do in our hearts and with our tongues. May He help and strengthen all men in every good endeavor...May we never forget that in the sunshine of our lives, through the storm and after the rain—it is all with God—in all ways and forever." Then in all capital letters he concludes, "ALL PRAISE TO GOD."

The album is significantly divided into four parts which he felt defined the steps on the path to spiritual enlightenment. These steps were "Acknowledgment," "Resolution," "Pursuance" and "Psalm." One could argue that they define the periods in his life after the rebirth experienced in 1957. In 1957 he "acknowledged" the presence of God and made a "resolution" to "pursue" the path which would move him closer to God. Viewed this way, the years after 1957 were years of the pursuance of a technique and style, and of fellow travelers along the path to enlightenment.

In December of 1964, with the recording of *A Love Supreme*, these years of pursuance come to an end; the final period of "psalm" begins. Thoreau once said that music is continuous and that only listening to it is intermittent. By 1965, Trane was hearing continuous music, as if *A Love Supreme* had lifted the last barriers holding back this continuous flow of music. Now it poured into his life, saturating all corners of it, like gushing water from some great broken dam.

Throughout his life he had listened for and heard parts of this mysterious music. He heard it in Stravinsky's "Firebird Suite" and its use of the double diminished scale in the late forties; during the sheets of sound period with Miles Davis; in the complex harmonic sounds of *Giant Steps*; in the strange harp-like sounds during his engagement with Monk at the Five Spot; in the mysterious droning sound of 1957 while pulling away from addiction; in the modal, chant-like music from the East, and in the music of the ancient African Griots which told the history of a race through rhythm.

But as important as these sounds were, they were only intermittent comings and goings of the great ocean of continuous music which he suspected existed somewhere behind and around all of them. The different sounds he had heard over his career were musical portholes offering him brief glimpses of the great sea outside the ship he traveled through life on. He could briefly hear some of the roar of the great ocean in the distance, but soon the musical windows were gone and he would move on, searching for other ways to reach the pure music behind them. The parts always seemed to exist separately with little blending. Coltrane learned certain lessons along the way and approximated certain sounds, but there was little attempt to fit these pieces of the great puzzle together. He simply filed them away for future reference.

With *A Love Supreme*, Coltrane brought forth all of the

individual pieces and blended them together. In the process they lost their distinction as partial approximations of the great continuous sound, and in fact became the sound. The great sound surrounds Coltrane, permeating every cell of his existence, and he becomes a medium for it. Everything was sacred and worthy only of expression in the awestruck hushed reverence of psalm.

The atmosphere around him was now fresh and clear like the weather after a great tropical storm, and he saw life in a new perspective. There was now a strong and forceful clarity to everything in his life. This is the central feeling one arrives at after listening to the music of this period. Only a handful of jazz critics seemed to have a clue as to what was happening. They continued to assign values to the music and reduce it to a manageable size. But as Albert Camus once remarked, "Where lucidity reigns, a scale of values becomes unnecessary." With Trane in 1965, lucidity reigned.

The music of this period communicated the lucidity to others in a spectacularly successful effort. William James once remarked that we are all victims of habit neurosis. He meant that our perceptions are dulled by the daily habit of living in a structured environment. With sharp, jarring sounds Coltrane attempts to wake the sleeping populace from this habitual neurosis. With a new, fresh, unusual sound he attempts to shock listeners out of this habitual existence and make them feel something unique for the first time.

He wasn't the only one carrying out this experiment. In

the rolling desert of northern Mexico, a Yaqui Indian sorcerer named Don Juan attempted to break the habit neurosis of a young apprentice named Carlos Castaneda. In the United States an angry young man named Jim Morrison beckoned us to "break on through to the other side." A rock musician named Jimi Hendrix tried to electrically capture the psychedelic vision.

While Coltrane wasn't the only one attempting to communicate a new vision of the world, he was one of the few who fully explored the methods of communication in the process. How could the awesome scenery of his personal geography be communicated to others with the least amount of change between the original experience and the communicated experience? This was a primary concern. If it was communicated as roughly as possible, it might wake parts of the sleeping populace.

Some believed that communication was most effective through the eye of a color television camera or through the ingestion of massive doses of drugs. Or through moving pictures. Or perhaps by stringing words together. Theories bounced around like hundreds of ping pong balls. Trane never subscribed to any of the theories because he saw very clearly that life's experiences can best be explored and communicated through those invisible vibrations of sound called music. The key seemed to be in the vibrations themselves. Through vibrations the sound of a culture's "collective unconscious" might be captured and new experiences arrived at.

Coltrane may have been in contact with some universal

sound which had been passed down through the ages. In *Coltrane: A Biography*, C.O. Simpkins notes that he told others "I'm looking for a universal sound." In 1968, Alice Coltrane reflected on this period, saying "I think what he was trying to do in music was the same thing he was trying to do in his life. That was to universalize his music, his life, his religion. It was all based on a universal concept, all-sectarian or non-sectarian. In other words, he respected all faiths, all religious beliefs. In music it was the same way because he had such a combination of concepts and ideas, some interwoven with each other."

During this period he told Elvin Jones he believed a particular combination of notes would cause matter to fall away from itself. Throughout his house all sorts of books were scattered about, and his sax stayed with him everywhere he went. In ways it was like the time of *Giant Steps*, when he fell asleep with his horn in his mouth.

The universal sound Coltrane searched for during this time was related to the very core of music and the mystical nature of the octave from which music is created. The octave has been a concern to a number of mystics and philosophers throughout the ages, but it was particularly the concern of the Russian mystic G.I. Gurdjieff, who propounded a "law of octaves." In his book *In Search of the Miraculous* he relates that this law is the formula of a cosmic law worked out by ancient schools and applied to music. "In order to understand the meaning of this law it is necessary to regard the universe as consisting of vibrations. These vibrations proceed in all kinds, aspects, and densities of the matter which constitutes the universe, from the finest to the coarsest; they issue from various sources and proceed in various directions, crossing one another, colliding, strengthening, weakening, arresting one another, and so on."

Gurdjieff says that according to the usual views accepted in the West these vibrations are continuous. "This means that vibrations are usually regarded as proceeding uninterruptedly, ascending or descending so long as there continues to act the force of the original impulse which caused the vibration and which overcomes the resistance of the medium in which the vibrations proceed." As Gurdjieff notes, one of the fundamental propositions of Western physics is the "continuity of vibrations."

However, the view of ancient knowledge believes in the "discontinuity of vibrations." This principle states that the characteristic of all vibrations in nature, whether ascending or descending, is to develop not uniformly but with periodic accelerations and retardations. Gurdjieff remarks that "The force of the impulse acts without changing its nature and vibrations develop in a regular way only for a certain time which is determined by the nature of the impulse, the medium, the conditions, and so forth. But at a certain moment a kind of change takes place in it and the vibrations, so to speak, cease to obey it and for a short time they slow down and to a certain extent change their nature and direction." To Gurdjieff this is significant because these periods of uniform action of momentum are not equal and the moments of retardation of the vibrations are not symmetrical. "One period is shorter, the other is longer."

The "discontinuity of vibrations" led to the discovery of the octave in music. For in order to determine the moments of retardation and the checks in the ascent and the descent of vibrations, the lines of development of vibrations are divided into periods corresponding to the doubling or the halving of the vibrations in a given space of time. The period in which vibrations are doubled was divided into eight unequal steps corresponding to the rate of increase in the vibrations, the eighth step repeating the first step with double the number of vibrations. Each period has seven distinct changes of vibration and is termed an octave. "In this way," Gurdjieff concludes, "was obtained the seven-tone musical scale."

Whether Trane was familiar with Gurdjieff's ideas at this time is unclear and at the same time unimportant. The ideas of Gurdjieff and others about the vibratory nature of the universe serve to place what he was doing at this time in a larger perspective rather than to explain it. We do know that during this period he was reading many books on mysticism and the occult. He received great assistance from his readings of the *Kabbala*, the basis for a particular type of Jewish mysticism, when he was composing *A Love Supreme*.

And we do know that he was thinking about vibrations and their relationship to life. In the August 14, 1965, issue of *Melody Maker* magazine he says, "I want to get to a point where I can feel the vibrations of a particular place at a particular moment and compose a song right there, on the spot."

Sometimes, though, the constant and continuous vibrations were too much for him. In August 1965, he and Alice moved out of New York City and into a modern house built on three acres of land in Dix Hills, Huntington, Long Island, where he spent the remainder of his life. He had wanted to leave the city for many years because of the constant "vibration" he felt in the ground.

Part Three
Spirit

Possession

The period ushered in by the vibrations of *A Love Supreme* brought a second rebirth. It was a multifaceted rebirth, though. If it possessed an overriding spiritual congruity it was a force which appeared in various guises—or disguises—throughout this period. At times it was wild and emotional like the spirit present in the Reverend Blair's church back in High Point, North Carolina, in the thirties. Other times it was quiet and reflective like the period around Miles Davis' *Kind of Blue* and the mood of "All Blues" from the album. Sometimes it was a force which bravely forged into frontier territory. Totally new things were encountered on the journey, many times unexpectedly, like an artistic ambush in the wilderness comprising the frontier of an art form.

Alice Coltrane remembers the first part of 1965 was good. "John was working on ideas, on structures, that would lead into the further freeing of time and textures that characterized his final period. He was doing a lot of writing, even more writing than practicing." It was an exciting time for him, like being on a funhouse ride with new forms and shapes popping up in brilliant illumination all about him all the time.

Nat Hentoff notes "He could never know exactly when

a door to perception would open, and that's why he was always in a state of preparation—practicing, writing, working out ideas." Alice Coltrane recalls that when he left for work, he would often take five instruments with him, including two or three tenors, so that he would be ready for whatever came.

During the first few months of 1965 not much came. On February 17 and 18 he recorded two originals, "Brazilia" and "Song of Praise," and two standards, "Nature Boy" and "Chim Chim Cheree" on *The John Coltrane Quartet Plays*. For the most part the unoriginality in the album's title matches the unoriginality in the album's content. Most of it is a reworking of some earlier ideas such as the Eastern sound he was searching for in the early sixties.

The next recording date, March 28th, yields *The New Wave in Jazz*, containing the sole piece "Nature Boy" written in the forties by Eden Ahbez and made famous by Nat King Cole. It describes a wise boy who wanders over land and sea in search of the truth and finds that the greatest thing is to love and be loved in return. As Bill Cole notes in *John Coltrane*, "Trane begins the piece right at that very point in the song." Later in the piece, Cole observes, "Trane is very searching in his solo, and his sound has more vibrato and is even more Eastern than on *A Love Supreme*." The music "was a far cry from *A Love Supreme*," Cole says, "and it is apparent that his research had taken him into another place—working more in small areas and developing and spinning lines off those small phrases."

A silence of two months fell over his recording career.

Then, from May 26 through June 28, he recorded seven new compositions which eventually found their way onto four new albums. The music flowed continuously during this time and he seemed in touch again with that mysterious and universal sound.

The first piece of the creative barrage was "Dear Lord," recorded on May 26. More than any other composition during his career, "Dear Lord" shows he had reached a certain state of serenity and found it necessary to express his thanks to God for this welcome deliverance. It is constructed from a surprisingly simple two-note motif, but this simplicity is at the core of the composition's strength. All of the excess improvisational luggage is jettisoned along with all the harmonic tricks and the melodic and rhythmic devices. What remains is a sparse, wintry sound which stands against nature's forces like a stately old Victorian mansion along the treeless Mendocino coast of northern California. The piece "Welcome," recorded a month later on June 28, pairs the two compositions that represent a final resting place for Trane before the onslaught of an artistic possession which would soon take hold of him for the rest of his life.

This possession begins two weeks after "Dear Lord" with the compositions "Transition" and "Suite" recorded on June 10. Nat Hentoff finds them a contrast to "Dear Lord," stating that where "Dear Lord" is "an expression of a transient serenity" these two pieces are "fired by discovery" evidencing "so propulsive a joy in the very act of searching and finding forms" for expression. Alice

Coltrane reflects about this time that "There was never any settling in for John," that he was "always moving ahead, looking for new avenues."

On "Transition" this search for new avenues is readily apparent. At over fifteen minutes, it is one of the longest pieces in the Coltrane discography. Like most of his other long pieces, spontaneity reigns over composition. Apart from the first few minutes used to state the theme, it is mostly a spontaneous piece finding a certain precedent in the material around the live Village Vanguard date in November of 1961 and especially the piece "Chasin' the Trane."

As the title implies, Trane was in an incredible state of transition during June of 1965 and it comes through in his music. He runs the notes through his horn at supersonic speed, in some ways similar to his sheets of sound period with Miles Davis. But since that earlier period he has learned much and does not get trapped down dead-end streets like he used to. The frenzied music continually expands outward, actively seeking and confronting what may be out there. The courageousness of the assault is one of the central feelings one takes away from the piece.

"Suite," recorded the same day as "Transition," is a vivid premonition. Divided into five parts, it addresses itself to the different times during the day that Trane used for prayer and meditation. There is "Prayer and Meditation: Day," "Prayer and Meditation: Evening" and "Prayer and Meditation: 4:00 a.m."

A number of things can be said about the music of

"Suite." One is that it represents the first of a string of compositions beginning in 1965 which the Coltrane "uninitiated" would find hard to listen to. Even his following from the Atlantic label found it an unusual metamorphosis for their old hero. Based around a simple triplet figure, the music has no central rhythm in the traditional sense but is rather spun out from the thundering drum rolls of Elvin Jones. In the background, Tyner dances up and down the keyboard creating a harp-like ethereal sound. Here and there Tyner punctuates his playing with strong keys in the bass and these serve to demarcate new plateaus reached or new plateaus to strive for. They are reminders to Coltrane that there was still farther to go.

In this interplay a tension is created which many listeners find unnerving. He may not now be guilty of getting caught down musical deadends but, at the same time, he seldom explores one street long enough to run up against deadends. Awe and ecstasy overpower his compositional abilities, smothering them in a volcanic eruption of sound as the tension mounts.

Around ten minutes into "Suite" something unusual happens when McCoy Tyner explodes on the piano with powerful playing offering a premonition of his musical future. For a few minutes Tyner steps away from his foundational function in the group and becomes the power source—in effect, an Elvin Jones of the piano. Styles which would find maturity in the seventies quickly flash by, and underneath the emerging styles there is Tyner's constant strong, melodic, lyrical voice. It is a power drawn from a deep inner reservoir of energy. When Coltrane returns his outlook has been touched by McCoy's vision and he responds with some of the most overwhelming music of his life. The tension is finally released.

Less than a week later, on June 16, Trane recorded one of the strongest statements of his career with the composition "Living Space." The frantic pace and exploding spontaneity of "Transition" and "Suite" give way to a slow, deliberate pace emphasizing melodic simplicity. In its brooding manner and harsh style, Coltrane creates an air of apprehension which serves as a dramatic counterpoint to the rest of his 1965 music.

The apprehension was justified by reference to the changes taking place in the world and in America. The war in Vietnam was escalating and fighting was breaking out between India and Pakistan. And two months after "Living Space" was recorded, the worst racial riot in American history broke out in the Watts section of Los Angeles. The tension in the American atmosphere was superbly translated into music with "Living Space."

The incredible burst of creativity in June 1965 concluded on June 28 with "Ascension," "Vigil" and "Welcome." This trio of compositions, arguably some of the most significant works of his career, serves to place his artistic struggles in bold relief. In this sense each of these compositions shows an inner side of Coltrane fighting for outward expression, for domination over the others, for that elusive artistic synthesis.

"Ascension" from *Ascension* has been called his boldest

attempt at spontaneous improvisation. As such it was the realization of a dream that he had since 1961 of recording in a large band setting where everyone played without reference to chords. For the experiment to be successful, he assembled the cream of a controversial new group of musicians who were exploring free form in jazz. This jazz movement of the mid-sixties was called the "New Thing" and most of the important young players, like Freddie Hubbard, Dewey Johnson, Marion Brown, Archie Shepp, Pharoah Sanders, Art Davis and John Tchicai, were all part of the new movement. All of them appear on "Ascension."

Marion Brown comments on the album's liner notes: "We did two takes and they both had that kind of thing in them that makes people scream. The people who were in the studios were screaming. I don't know how the engineers kept the scream out of the record. Spontaneity was the thing."

Most of the music for *Ascension* was written in the studio on recording day. Coltrane told everybody what he wanted. He played a certain line and told everyone to play that line in the ensemble. He was attempting to mix spontaneity and composition at the same time and arrive at a new unity.

As Archie Shepp commented, "It achieves a certain kind of unity; it starts at a high level of intensity with the horns playing high and the other pieces low. This gets a quality like male and female voices. It builds in intensity through all the solo passages, brass and reeds, until it gets to the final section where the rhythm section takes over and brings it back to the level it started at. The idea is similar to what painters do in that it creates various surfaces of color which push into each other, creating tensions and counter tensions, and various fields of energy."

In this way the music on *Ascension* might be visualized as various colors of thick, luminescent oils constantly shifting into new patterns within some form of container. The image of the popular lava lamps of this period comes to mind. Archie Shepp notes that "The ensemble passages were based on chords. But these chords were optional. What Trane did was to relate or juxtapose tonally centered ideas and atonal elements, along with melodic and non-melodic elements. In those descending chords, there is a definite tonal center, like B-flat minor. But there are different roads to that center...The emphasis was on textures rather than the making of an organizational entity." In a certain sense the music was a modernized extension of Dixieland jazz into a big band setting.

If *Ascension* represented the overall tone of Coltrane's mood and emerging ideas during this period, the compositions "Vigil" and "Welcome" from *Kulu Sé Mama* represented the two great forces which fought for control of his life: the force of tranquillity and peacefulness reached when a destination was arrived at and the force of agitated watchfulness and movement while on the path to the destination.

On the album's liner notes Coltrane offers the best explanation of these two forces, noting that "vigil implies watchfulness. Anyone trying to obtain perfection is faced with various obstacles in life which tend to sidetrack him…I mean watchfulness against the elements that might be destructive from within and without. I don't try to set standards of perfection for anyone else. I do feel everyone does try to reach his better self, his full potential, and what that consists of depends on each individual. Whatever the goal is, moving toward it does require vigilance." On the other hand Coltrane observes that "welcome is that feeling you have when you finally do reach awareness, an understanding which you have earned through struggle. It is a feeling of peace. A welcome feeling of peace." The two compositions offer additional evidence of the struggle between the two great extremes of his life.

In 1965, John Coltrane was not alone in trying to resolve these extremes. The dual forces of peace and vigil seemed to permeate the American atmosphere and push at each other like the musical patterns from "Ascension." Neither one dominated, though, and in this unresolved interaction it was difficult to tell whether something great was growing or something great was maybe dying.

It was a year filled with many strange juxtapositions. In January, Lyndon Johnson took the oath of office for his first full term as president and Winston Churchill died in London. In February, the war in Vietnam expanded as America began air attacks on North Vietnam. In April, fighting broke out between India and Pakistan and a civil war began in the Dominican Republic. In July, Adlai Stevenson died in London, and in September Albert Schweitzer died. In October, the New York World's Fair closed, and in November a great power failure blacked out parts of the northeastern United States and Canada. Above these events spacecraft with names like Ranger, Gemini and Mariner circled the earth or headed into outer space toward the moon or Mars.

The transition taking place in America was probably best documented in rock'n'roll music. The age of innocence and peace of early rock'n'roll was changing into a period of watchfulness and vigilance, and the change was becoming increasingly evident in rock music. The Who were smashing guitars on stage and talking about "Our Generation" and Jim Morrison was beckoning young people to "Break On Through" to the other side. Jimi Hendrix saw the strange atmosphere of the time as a "Purple Haze" and in San Francisco there was Janis Joplin's Big Brother and Gracie Slick's Jefferson Airplane.

But it is in the music of the English Beatles that this shift in American attitudes is best documented. The early albums such as *Introducing The Beatles, The Beatles, A Hard Day's Night* and *Something New* from 1964 addressed themselves to a number of teenage problems and concerns such as being in love and finding the right girl. Songs such as "She Loves You" and "I Saw Her Standing There" are good illustrations of these early Beatles concerns.

By 1965, these themes began to move into the background of their music as it became more obtuse and complex, with deeper concerns. On the album *Help* the group echoed the cries of many young people to "help me get my feet back on the ground." *Rubber Soul* followed *Help* and moved them still further away from their initial music. By

1966, things have changed so much from their early days at the Cavern Club in Liverpool that they now looked back nostalgically on those years with a sadness in their music. On *Yesterday And Today* from 1966 Paul laments that "Yesterday all my troubles seemed so far away, now I know they're here to stay." The words expressed the sentiments of many Americans—the yesterday Paul sang about was the American innocence which had ended in the 1950s. And in the drug-induced "purple haze" of the emerging new culture it was still impossible to see what shapes loomed ahead.

While the Beatles gave popular expression to America's fading innocence, the forces of the times raged their most intense battles inside Coltrane's music. They were battles that leaders of rock'n'roll were closely monitoring to see if it had application to rock. For the first time, major communication developed between the two forms, and John Coltrane was increasingly viewed as a visionary.

John McLaughlin was one of the musicians greatly influenced by Coltrane's music. He remembers "Once as I was listening to *Ascension* I went into a kind of trance and saw myself flying over Africa. I could feel the spirit of the entire continent and its pulsating, teeming life; I could hear African music and Coltrane's music simultaneously. But I couldn't see the people; only the jungle and savannas, even though I was no more than fifty feet above the ground. It was John Coltrane's music that carried me there, as if he was leading me by the hand." In the late 1960s McLaughlin would be one of the major architects of a new music called jazz-rock fusion.

The leader of the well-known Byrds was also very influenced by Coltrane. Roger McGuinn observes that "I loved flying, and Trane's music gives me the feeling of flying. It scares me and thrills me, just as flying does." In the summer of 1965, when the Byrds were touring the country and traveling in a mobile home, they had only two cassettes to serenade them. One of the cassettes included Ravi Shankar ragas and the other cassette featured the Coltrane compositions "Africa" and "India." McGuinn suggested working in some of Coltrane's phrases and the result is heard on their memorable recording "Eight Miles High." As McLaughlin says, "The first break is a direct quote from a Coltrane phrase, and throughout the rest of the song we try to emulate the scales and modes that Trane was using. Especially his spiritual feeling, which got me into transcendental meditation not long afterwards."

The feelings of McLaughlin and McGuinn are echoed by Gracie Slick and Carlos Santana. Of the *Meditations* album recorded in November of 1965, Santana says, "I haven't heard anything higher than 'The Father and the Son and the Holy Ghost'...I would often play it at four in the morning...I could hear God's mind in that music, influencing John Coltrane. I heard the Supreme One playing music through John Coltrane's mind."

A significant trend toward Indian music entered rock music around 1965. Again, this shift is best documented for the majority of Americans in the music of the Beatles, which takes on an increasing Indian technique and perspective with songs such as the 1965 "Norwegian Wood" and albums such as the 1967 *Sergeant Pepper's Lonely Hearts Club Band* and *Magical Mystery Tour,* and the 1969 *Yellow Submarine* and *Abbey Road.* During this period, George Harrison and all of the Beatles were intensely studying the Indian sitar, and particularly the music of Ravi Shankar.

Coltrane was also studying Shankar's music, and in November of 1965 he met Shankar. It was an important but relatively unnoticed event in the music world with consequences never fully explored. Of course Coltrane had been fascinated by music of the Near East most of his life, an interest sparked in the early fifties during his friendship with Yusef Lateef, an interest which would weave itself in and out of his music on works such as "My Favorite Things," *Impressions* and *Africa/Brass.*

By 1965, his concern was increasingly with the music of India and the Far East and specifically with the music of the legendary Ravi Shankar. For it was in the music of Shankar that the deep heritage of Indian music found a contemporary translator. The respect Coltrane had for Shankar is evident in much of the music from 1965. It is also evident by the Coltranes naming their second son, born in August of 1965, Ravi, after Ravi Shankar. The two had not met but respect was growing between them.

In November of 1965, after the exchange of many letters and experiences, Shankar and Coltrane finally met in New York, where Shankar was appearing in concert. Shankar recalls the event, saying "Meeting John was a great surprise. Most jazz musicians I have met were not interested in anything outside of their own musical world, but here was a humble and self-effacing man with an interest in other people and their cultures like few I have ever met." They had dinner together and the next day discussed music and demonstrated certain musical techniques to each other. Most of the time, at Coltrane's request, was taken up with Ravi's discussion of his country's musical heritage.

The discussion fascinated and meant a great deal to Coltrane, for in the sitar playing of Shankar he heard that majestic, sweeping harp sound he had heard parts of through much of his life. It was like being enveloped under magnificent waves of continuous music; he wanted to learn everything he could about it and add it to his music.

Ravi Shankar was different from Coltrane in one major respect. In Shankar the two forces of peace and chaos, of arrival and watchfulness, did not wage that violent interior battle they waged in Coltrane. Shankar was a man of inward peace, but it was a peace he did not find in his friend Coltrane's music. "The music was fantastic," he says about hearing Coltrane at the Village Gate in November 1965. "I was much impressed. But one thing distressed me. There was a turbulence in the music that gave me a negative feeling at times, but I could not quite put my finger on the trouble."

This turmoil is harshly evident on Coltrane's albums from August, September, October and November of 1965. Within these four months the opposing forces of his life raged as never before. The result is uniquely different music no one had ever heard.

In August 1965, on *Sun Ship*, the turmoil is particularly evident in the pieces "Sunship" and "Amen." Critic Bill Cole views the music from *Sun Ship* as "unquestionably the most open, fresh music" the quartet had ever done. This perspective is not difficult to see, but at the same time there is a great agitated force within "Sunship," something like the frantic efforts of an angry hornet to escape from a jar.

It had happened before in his music, but never with this new sense of intensity and power. The tension between Coltrane and Tyner is awesome, created largely by Coltrane's use of triplets. Charged by an initial explosion of these musical figures, Tyner is inspired to play some of the most brilliant music of his career. As he did in "Suite" from June of 1965, he again takes a position of control and pushes the quartet to new limits.

Unfortunately, after August of 1965, these limits were never explored by the John Coltrane Quartet. The band was beginning to break up. By February of 1966, all of the original members were gone except Garrison.

As before, a period of transition was pushing Trane's music onto a new plateau. The plateau was still taking shape, but it was becoming evident to Trane that he needed to have other types of musicians to create the sound he heard. It was a difficult time. The quartet had been closer than a family and there was a great sadness in Trane as his family began to break up.

• • •

It is perhaps this feeling of impending separation that fires much of the music from the last months of 1965. On September 22, 1965, the quartet records "Joy," their final piece together. After this date the band became a revolving-door band with new musicians constantly coming and going through it during Coltrane's final two years of life.

So it seems appropriate that in the composition "Joy" the forces pulling at Trane are all uniquely brought together in some of the most haunting music he ever made. The music is hypnotic and Trane's horn sounds like some Pied Piper, maintaining a subtle, wavering balance between the forces of peace and exploration. An underlying sense of ecstasy and exultation creates an emotional power which continues to grow as the forces of order and chaos are kept in check by Coltrane's powerful horn.

A week after recording "Joy," the group went to Seattle, Washington, to play a date at The Penthouse. Significantly, two new members were added to the original quartet to make a sextet. These new additions ushered in Trane's revolving-door bands. One of the new additions was Donald Garrett on bass clarinet and the other was Pharoah Sanders on tenor sax. Garrett recorded three more albums with Trane.

Pharoah Sanders, though, offered something more to Coltrane than another band member. At a time when Trane's musical family was drifting apart Pharoah became a strong, final force in Trane's life. It might be said that Coltrane nurtured three young players during his life, drawing heavily on their music and spiritual strength at critical periods when he found himself drained and in need of fresh inspiration to move ahead. The musicians greatly grew under their apprenticeships and became like sons to him. The musicians were Eric Dolphy, McCoy Tyner and Pharoah Sanders. Dolphy was now gone and Tyner was in the process of leaving. But in September 1965, the apprenticeship and friendship of Sanders was just beginning.

Pharoah Sanders is first heard on record with Trane at the live dates of September 30 and October 1 at The Penthouse in Seattle. From the music of these two nights came the albums *Live in Seattle* and *Om*. Both contain some of the strangest music he ever played. Critic Bill Cole remarks about "Cosmos" and "Evolution" from *Live in Seattle* that it was music of "such great introspection that I believe it is where Trane became his most visionary." This is partly true, for there are incredible peaks of excitement in the music, but also long tedious stretches which only seem to drift. Excitement and tedium continually mix in the Seattle music.

A major reason for the tedium was that Trane and Garrett took LSD before recording *Om*. It was a new experience for Trane and his reaction to the experience may have produced the mystical and eerie vibrations heard throughout the album. Included in the mysterious music was the chanting of selected verses from the *Bhagavad Gita*. His comment after the experience was that "I perceived the interrelationship of all life forms."

Om is a strange album finding its closest predecessor in the music from *Ascension*. Like *Ascension*, the music on *Om* is of a unified composition, a swirling, changing vortex of sound patterns constantly expanding outward and spreading like a type of raging virus. However one views this album it finally converted Nat Hentoff, that perennial critic who had been attacking Coltrane through scathing articles in *Down Beat*. On the liner notes to *Om* Hentoff wrote some of the most praiseworthy notes of his long career as one of America's foremost jazz critics.

Admittedly the album is difficult to listen to. But on the liner notes Hentoff implores the listener not to worry about "how it is all structured, where it's leading. Let the music come in without any pre-set definitions of what jazz has to be, of what music has to be." He notes that in listening to the music "emotions are the way into this music rather than intellectual diagrams or quick categorical guidelines by which you have evaluated jazz in the past." Once one lets emotions take over, Hentoff says, an entirely new world awaits the listener. Writing with the intensity of a newly converted disciple, he observes, "One of the most durable values of Coltrane's music is that if you stay with it, it drives you beneath the surface layers into a qualitatively different way of hearing the interrelationships of sounds, including pitches."

Hentoff concludes his long liner notes to *Om* by writing "As one listener, I can attest that I get from it a sense of the limitlessness of what music can express and, thereby, of what man can express...For there was no way to predict what would happen, and although there were past experiences to act as a bridge to the start of each new adventure, once that adventure began, I was on my own. And that, I believe, is what John Coltrane intended for all his listeners."

The seminal year of 1965 ends with *Kulu Sé Mama* and *Meditations*, both extremely different from each other and from the music recorded in Seattle. They demonstrate the wide range of Trane's music. *Kulu Sé Mama*, recorded in Los Angeles in October, is one of Coltrane's longest pieces. The poet Juno Lewis mumbles a strange ritualistic chant throughout. The movement toward African cultural heritage is apparent through Trane's use of two drummers. Lewis plays the water drum and we can hear an immediate similarity with the sound from *Africa/Brass*. Only now the music is more sophisticated as rhythm again becomes Coltrane's main concern.

In November the forces of composition temporarily gained control over Trane's life and he recorded one of the great three suites of his career. On November 23 the album *Meditations* was recorded in New York. In its organizational unity and overall vision it pulled together many of the disparate forces which raged for control over Coltrane during 1965.

The remarks of Trane to Hentoff on the liner notes of *Meditations* are interesting and instructive. "There is never any end," he tells Hentoff. "There are always new sounds to imagine; new feelings to get at. And always, there is the need to keep purifying these feelings and sounds so that we can really see what we've discovered in its pure state. So that we can see more clearly what we are. In that way, we can give those who listen the essence, the best of what we are."

Coltrane then makes a comment that helps explain his increasing involvement with the radical young players in constantly changing recording contexts. He says to keep hearing the new sounds and experiencing the new feelings a constant purification is necessary. "We have to keep cleaning the mirror," he says. The music from the final two years of his life is created from this perspective. With mysterious sounds constantly bombarding him, it seemed necessary to work with different musicians and musical contexts to keep the "mirror" clean.

Peace

A s 1966 began to unfold, Coltrane was at the pinnacle of his career. In 1965 *Down Beat* magazine proclaimed Coltrane "Jazzman of the Year" and elected him to the Hall of Fame. He was also awarded first place on tenor saxophone in *Down Beat*'s annual poll, while *A Love Supreme* was named Record of the Year.

The money he made from his recording contract with Impulse and with Jowcol, his own publishing company, is estimated at approximately $200,000 a year. With this money he bought a large twelve-room house on three acres of land in Dix Hills, Huntington, Long Island. The property included a large garden which he worked in constantly. The home fulfilled a long-held dream of leaving the city.

Behind the house was a forest and in front a high wrought iron gate. The inside was filled with various types of art and a variety of instruments: a grand piano, an Indian sitar, conga drums, a small African horn, bagpipes, flutes and a number of saxophones. There was also the bass clarinet of Eric Dolphy, a gift from Dolphy's mother. He had come a long way from the little house in High Point and the tiny room in Philadelphia.

Yet despite his popularity and success he was increasingly possessed by that strange music he did not understand. It seemed he was becoming a type of medium, losing control over the direction of his music. There was constant experimentation with new techniques, new mouthpieces and exotic technical devices like the Varitone electronic saxophone attachment. These experiments were conducted with constantly changing sidemen and he could never fully anticipate the kind of music a performance would produce. Trane had surprised his audiences with technique, but now he began to surprise them with totally new musical forms.

In February of 1966 he entered the studio after a two month hiatus from the intense work of 1965. Tyner and Jones were gone, replaced by Alice Coltrane on piano and Rashied Ali on drums. Pharoah Sanders was on tenor sax and flute, Ray Appleton on percussion, and Joan Chapman on tamboura. The only vestige of the original Coltrane quartet was Jimmy Garrison on bass.

The result was *Cosmic Music,* and it serves as a good illustration of the strange new music Coltrane was attempting to express. An increased interest in rhythm is apparent from his use of Ali, Chapman and Appleton. However, his concern is not with the traditional rhythm which moves a composition forward but rather with an all-encompassing rhythm which pervades the musical atmosphere. A drone sound provides a constant background hum. It is close to the sound he had heard for years.

The four compositions on *Cosmic Music* make up the entire list of Coltrane's original work for 1966. It was a year that saw the creation of only three albums. This fact becomes significant when one considers that 1965 produced eleven albums and almost twenty-five original pieces.

He seemed confused. This confusion surfaced later in February during a reunion with an old friend and teacher at Cobo Hall in Detroit. At Cobo Hall he shared the bill with Thelonious Sphere Monk; it was their first appearance together in almost ten years. Due to an unusual all-day snowstorm, Trane's rhythm section was snowed in and only Trane and Alice were there. George Wein, producer of the concert, asked Trane if he would mind playing with Monk to close out the concert and Trane said yes, of course, yes. Upon hearing this, Monk immediately danced his approval and gave Trane a big affectionate hug.

They played mostly Monk's music, in particular those tunes from their 1957 collaboration. Afterward, in the dressing room, Trane was in a pensive mood and said to Wein, "You know, I often wonder whether what I'm doing now is the right way to play. Sometimes I feel this is the way I want to go, but other times I'd rather return to the way I used to play." Wein recalls that Trane then paused and added, "But for now, I think I'll continue in the direction I'm going and see what happens."

In March, Elvin Jones, who had played sporadically with Trane since November 1965 and the arrival of Rashied Ali, gave his final notice to Trane. They had just finished one week of a two-week engagement at San Francisco's Jazz Workshop and Elvin gave abrupt notice that he was leaving to join Duke Ellington in Europe. Elvin commented on the direction of Coltrane's music that "Only poets can understand it."

In July of 1966, after a live recording date at the Village Vanguard which produced *Live At The Village Vanguard Again*, the group went to Japan for an extremely successful tour. The Japanese idolized Coltrane, which was evident from large mobs following the group everywhere. If the Europeans considered Trane an artist, the Japanese considered him a brother.

Alice remembers a touching incident which shows the respect and admiration of the Japanese for Trane. "John gave out a lot of autographs after our first Tokyo concert," she recalls. "Just as we were getting into our cab to leave, a young boy came running up but the driver pulled away too fast for him. He was still running when we were blocks away. Then, after we were back in the hotel room for about twenty minutes, we heard this knock at the door. It was this Japanese boy, who had apparently run all the way. He had followed us for miles just to get John's autograph."

Coltrane was stunned by this warm, loving reception. A photo shows the group's arrival in Tokyo on July 8. Trane holds a bouquet of flowers and humbly looks down. Behind him a huge banner proclaims "Welcome to Japan/John Coltrane Quintet." He is clearly surprised by the reception.

During a number of memorable concerts in the next two weeks, he demonstrated his appreciation to them. Toward the end of the tour, a live concert date was recorded on July 22 in Tokyo. The music found its way onto record as *Concert in Japan*. Like a number of his successful

1965 experiments, the music reached peaks of visionary brilliance interspersed with tedious solo flights between himself and Pharoah Sanders. Both are almost telepathic on the album and the interaction is a high point of Pharoah Sanders' career.

Despite the Japanese idolization of Coltrane, many Japanese critics did not understand the new music. Their idolization was not based on the late music but on the music around 1959, the "old" Coltrane. Writing in the Japanese jazz magazine *Swing Journal*, Yukitaka Tsutsui noted, "Coltrane has the power to impress the audience with simple melodic lines. But his sound is so insistent that I feel confusion and depression in his music. There is too much reality in his music for me to bear when I hear it, and I do not usually listen to music to hear these things in it." Shinichro Nakamaya observed, "I hear emotional excitement and passion in Coltrane's music, but I do not feel it as intensely as I expected to. His music is like a religious ceremony, not yet established but still changing and growing. It is not completely fulfilled yet." And the critic Yagi comments, "Both Coltrane and Sanders keep repeating the same phrases all the time. I think they are playing more for themselves than for the audience."

But for Coltrane the two weeks spent in Japan was one of the best times in his life. He felt a deep admiration for the Japanese culture. In many ways it represented that state of peace he was searching for in life and music. The Japanese seemed to be the living embodiment of the music from "Welcome." For a brief period he felt that he had finally arrived at a special destination in life. He expressed his gratitude in other ways than music to these tranquil people. On July 14 he prayed for the dead at the War Memorial Park in Nagasaki where the second atomic bomb of World War II was dropped, killing more than 150,000 Japanese.

However, the feeling of peace was only a temporary one. Something was seriously wrong with his health. The first inclinations of this were the terrible stomach pains he experienced during the Japanese tour. In one of the group's photos, Coltrane stands on a railway platform holding his stomach. George Wein remembers asking him to tour Europe in the fall. Coltrane told Wein he wasn't feeling well, that he was feeling weak. As Wein recalls, "he really sounded tired."

It was against this awakening suspicion of something terribly wrong that the music of his final year was created. The realization came to him at some point after July 1966. He knew his time was limited. He held personal appearances to a minimum and did not record an album for seven months after the Japanese concert. He began to brood heavily over things.

Ravi Shankar recalls, "I returned to New York at the end of 1966, and I called John at once. I invited him to visit me in India, and he said he would seriously consider my offer. He sounded very sad, and I told him I was disturbed after hearing the latest record he had sent me. He told me that he was feeling extremely frustrated, that he was still trying for something different, but he did not know what he was looking for."

He became increasingly involved with his close friend Babatunde Olatunji's African cultural center on 125th Street in Harlem. And he continued to use more controversial young musicians in his band. The critics wrote very negative reviews but Trane didn't seem to care. This was evidenced by a music which became stranger and stranger.

In December of 1966 he put together one of the most radical groups of his career at New York's Village Theater, later to become Bill Graham's Fillmore East. The session caused a number of members of the audience to walk out, but the response from the majority of the audience was enthusiastic shouting.

His final recording dates were in February and March of 1967 when he created music which, after being shuffled around by Impulse, became *Interstellar Space* and *Expression*. It represents the most unusual music of his career. In March of 1967 he recorded "Expression" and "Ogunde" on *Expression*, his last recorded works. *Interstellar Space* probably tops the list of Coltrane records which are difficult to listen to. By this time, there was great stomach pain and frequent severe headaches. His musical vision was now turned inward and away from current events. The eyes of the music world were still firmly focused on him, but now he was distant and alone, no longer part of the intricate, regular patterns of ordinary, everyday life.

In this state he seemed to shed everything. The compositions on *Interstellar Space*—"Mars," "Venus," "Jupiter" and "Saturn"—are raw and emotional, possessed with a distant unearthly quality, a cold, metallic character. The process of shedding the excess from his life has reduced the number of people accompanying him to only Rashied Ali on drums. With Ali he found a recipient of his final musical ideas, a musician who combined the percussion of the drums with intricate and complex multirhythms. He was a drummer ultimately free from the time structures of meter. Ali was that equal musical partner Trane had been searching for.

The interaction between the two musicians on *Interstellar Space* has the fury of a wild swarm of angry hornets. An intensity in the music keeps building and never lets up. Trane pursues ideas at supersonic speed, much like the sheets of sound period but now there is a cold finality about the pursuit. On "Venus" he achieves a totally new voice which springs out in jarring juxtapositions, as if Trane is possessed by different personalities.

In the midst of these turbulent final months, the end quickly approaching, there is a new beginning. On March 19 a third son is born to Trane and Alice. His name is Oran.

But the confusion grows. In April of 1967 he searched out the one great teacher in his life. On a visit to the city he went to Monk's apartment. He needed to see him. He waited an hour at Monk's until Monk came back. When Monk arrived they embraced warmly. Monk had always been a father to Coltrane. They went out onto Monk's terrace where fog blanketed the air and Trane told Monk in a distressed tone about the music he was making. Monk told him not to think about it but just to play it.

Next, there was confusion as Monk attempted to find

his hat for his engagement that night. Everyone looked all over for it until it was found. Trane was laughing. He loved this wonderful childlike quality of Monk. It was another of those marvelous Monk idiosyncrasies. Later that night he went down to the Vanguard to see Monk. It was a wonderful evening.

In May of 1967, he and Alice visited his mother in Philadelphia. One evening during the visit Trane suddenly clutched his stomach, staggered into the bedroom and closed the door. He was in extreme pain. Coming out of the bedroom an hour later he looked at his mother and wife as if neither of them were there in the house with him. Shortly after they returned to New York, Alice made an appointment with a stomach specialist. Upon examination by a doctor, he was ordered to stay in the hospital. He ignored the doctor's orders, though, and went home.

June and the first few weeks of July were filled with nightmarish pain. He got very little work accomplished. On July 14 Trane was in Bob Thiele's office at Impulse Records and left after discussing some business matters. Thiele recalls, "I got the distinct feeling that he was dying. I could see death on his face."

On Sunday morning, July 16, he was rushed to Huntington Hospital. He died there on Monday morning July 17, of primary hepatoma or cancer of the liver. He died at 4:00 a.m.—that special time of the day he used for meditation during the last few years.

It was the only time he was able to find a modicum of peace during these final few years.

Dawn

The Bible says portents of great changes appear through cataclysmic natural events. If this is true, this year has been a year full of portents.

In the spring a great mountain erupted with the most powerful explosion of the century. Within a few days the debris from the explosion spread over a large part of an entire continent. Passengers on a commercial airliner flying over the mountain saw a massive column of smoke rising sixty thousand feet into the sky towering over the height they were flying at. "It's a sight I'll never forget," says one of the airline passengers, her voice shaky, as if she has recently been touched by some revelation.

During the summer, large parts of the continent blistered under the worst heat in recorded history. Rich farmlands of corn and wheat were transformed into baked, cracked wastelands with surfaces harder than concrete. On this hard dry earth, animals lay dead by the thousands. In October the heat moved into the Bay Area and reached record highs. The sun hung over the city like a giant sun lamp with a pervasive heat impossible to escape. The weather was unusual because October is usually a moderate month for the Bay Area.

On one of October's boiling days I passed a nursing

home where elderly people sat on the porch rocking back and forth in green wicker chairs, fanning themselves, glancing at the white sun ball in the bone-white sky. For a moment it seemed the old people had the answers and were able to read the portents.

Across the bay, the outline of San Francisco shimmered in the curving waves of heat floating upward into a sky becoming hazy with smog rolling up from San Jose. In the waving mist San Francisco had an atmosphere like the film *Casablanca*. It lost its boundaries and appeared to be one great majestic mirage.

The record heat had a certain unifying effect and all around the Bay Area people were drawn outdoors and stood in front of their homes or stores and rubbed sweat off their necks and talked about the heat wave. There was speculation that the volcano in the spring caused the unusual weather.

Late in the summer's warm evenings, a radio evangelist warned that the end was near on a program broadcast out of Tyler, Texas. Biblical prophesy, he excitedly exclaimed, was being fulfilled. His voice was quick with short bursts of frenzied preaching, as if he didn't think there was much time left before a great approaching storm. Despite his excited emotional tone, there seemed to be a certain amount of truth in what he said.

Now, in December, the air is cool, the heat has left and the sky has changed from bleached bone-white to robin-egg blue. But even in this tranquil atmosphere, the portents remain in the atmosphere and one is again reminded of the peculiar yellowish color before the onslaught of the great tropical storms of Florida in the fifties.

If he was still with us John Coltrane could decipher the portents and help forecast the patterns of the future weather. John Lennon and Elvis Presley could also help decipher these portents. But these musical prophets are now gone and the world is overrun with false prophets crawling through every part of society like hungry termites, eating away at the very core of things, leaving only hollow shells of life in their destructive wake.

History is full of transitional periods between the end of one era and the beginning of another. These times take on that peculiar color of the atmosphere before tropical storms. In this atmosphere, the ordinary paths trampled on by all of us each day become difficult to see. Leaders emerge to help us again find the way. For many, these leaders come from the distinctly American art form of jazz. They are the ones who rescue us during these difficult periods.

In the forties and fifties jazz commanded the greatest rescue operations under Charlie Parker, Miles Davis and John Coltrane. In the sixties the musical power source shifted to rock'n'roll under the music of John Lennon and Elvis Presley. The seventies brought about an intermingling or "fusion" of jazz and rock, but instead of creating a powerful new synthesis the new music only created a bunch of strange mutations like disco, funk and punk. There was no John Coltrane, Charlie Parker, Elvis Presley or John Lennon. Music could not summon forth the magic it once possessed. The eighties and nineties saw rock and jazz homogenized and split into small segments, the music becoming little more nourishing than junk food.

Do we need to be rescued again? And will music once again play a major role in the rescue operations? Will it again produce the leaders it once produced? Will music once again become a great positive force in our lives?

On a cold December night I drive south down the interstate which runs along the eastern shore of the San Francisco Bay. Berkeley is on the left and San Francisco twinkles across the bay on the right like a great jumble of iridescent diamonds. Overhead the stars are dulled by a thick yellow moon which hangs among them like an old magic lantern.

The red light on top of the transmitting tower of the Berkeley jazz radio station blinks off and on to the left. The station is the last stronghold of progressive jazz radio in the Bay Area. It is a tenuous stronghold at best. Recently it was purchased by new owners from New York City and they are moving its programming away from the progressive jazz of Coltrane and Tyner to a "contemporary" easy-listening format. I have been involved with the Bay Area Jazz Society and there have been a number of meetings about this change but in the end there is little any of us can do. The new station owners tell us that the market out here just won't support a progressive jazz format.

I have a good friend who runs the late night jazz show on the radio station. With the new ownership of the station his time is limited and he has already started to pack his things to move on. Tonight I have his program on. He is playing "Impressions" from McCoy Tyner's *Trident* album. The famous Coltrane piece was recorded by Tyner in 1975 during a high-energy period of his career. It features Ron Carter on bass and Elvin Jones on drums.

It is one of Tyner's few trio recordings. This point is important because the interaction between the musicians on *Trident* is more readily apparent than on most other Tyner albums. Within this interaction dwells an approximation of that interaction which occurred on the original version of "Impressions" from Coltrane's famous Village Vanguard session. The opening lines of the piece explode at the listener in a strong, forceful manner, reaching higher and higher, working variations on the original Debussy line, examining it from different musical angles like Picasso examined objects in paintings.

Since John Coltrane's death in 1967, McCoy Tyner has undergone immense changes. Trane was like a father to him and Tyner took Trane's death very hard at first. But the initial feeling of overwhelming grief has eventually turned into a strong new voice—perhaps the most powerful spiritual voice in jazz.

A year after Trane's death this strong spiritual voice is already apparent in the Tyner composition "African Village." McCoy has almost single-handedly taken it upon himself to carry on the Coltrane torch. In the early seventies he teamed up with Orrin Keepnews at Milestone Records in Berkeley—the same Orrin Keepnews who originally produced Thelonious Monk on the Riverside label of the fifties. In many respects the relationship has been similar to that of John Coltrane and Bob Thiele of Impulse Records. The music they created through the seventies obtained a legendary status in the jazz world. Many of Coltrane's conceptions have been extended by Tyner and mixed with Tyner's growing sense of composition and orchestration.

As I drive along the edge of the San Francisco Bay tonight listening to Tyner play Coltrane's "Impressions," the realization comes that Trane's spirit is still with us. Like other great works of art, "Impressions" has outlasted its creator, becoming a high-energy jazz classic and an important part of the repertoire of numerous jazz groups across the nation. The piece seems to faithfully capture Coltrane's growing strength in the early 1960s and provides a vehicle for relaying this message to others.

From hotel lounges across America, to small jazz clubs in Greenwich Village or late night jazz radio stations in Berkeley, the Coltrane ideas are carried forth into the night of one era and toward the dawn of a new era. In 1824, James Morier wrote that "Every man you meet is either a descendant of the Prophet or a man of the law." McCoy Tyner is truly a "descendant of the Prophet."

The prophet was John Coltrane and Tyner's dedication to carry forth the Coltrane torch helps perpetuate his music into the dawn of a new era. The music of McCoy Tyner fills the night air and under an old yellow moon perhaps there is a new and powerful beginning and a new dawn in sight.

Bibliography

Berendt, Joachin. *The Jazz Book* (1953)

Case, Brian. *The Illustrated Encyclopedia of Jazz* (1978)

Chilton, John. *Who's Who In Jazz* (1978)

Cole, Bill. *John Coltrane* (1976)

Collier, James Lincoln. *The Making of Jazz* (1978)

Copland, Aaron. *The New Music* (1968)

Feather, Leonard. *The Book of Jazz* (1976)

Hentoff, Nat. *The Jazz Makers* (1957)

----------------------*Jazz* (1958)

----------------------*Jazz Is* (1972)

Hodeir, Andre. *Jazz: Its Evolution and Essence* (1956)

--------------------*The Worlds of Jazz* (1972)

Leonard, Neil. *Jazz: Myth and Religion* (1987)

Nisenson, Eric. *Ascension: John Coltrane and His Quest* (1993)

Simpkins, C.O. *Coltrane. A Biography* (1975)

Stearns, Marshall. *The Story of Jazz* (1956)

Thomas, J.C. *Chasin' the Trane* (1977)

Wild, David. *The Recordings of John Coltrane* (1978)

Williams, Martin. *The Meaning of Jazz* (1970)

Articles

Down Beat, December 26, 1957.

----------September 29, 1960.

----------November 23, 1961.

----------April 21, 1962.

----------August 27, 1964.

Jazz Review, November 1959.

Melody Maker, August 14, 1965.

Time, February 28, 1964.

Discography

(In chronological order)

Dizzy Gillespie And His Orchestra: Capitol 57797, 57839, 15852, 15611, 15849, 57892 (1949/1950)

Dizzy Gillespie Sextet: DeeGee 3600, 3601 (1951)

Earl Bostic And His Orchestra: King 4356, 4550, 4568, 4570 (1952)

Johnny Hodges And His Orchestra—Used To Be Duke: Verve 8150 (1954)

The New Miles Davis Quintet: Prestige 7254 (1955)

Paul Chambers—Jazz In Transition: Transition 30 (1955)

Paul Chambers: Jazz West 7 (1956)

John Coltrane With Hank Mobley—Two Tenors: Prestige 7670 (1956)

Miles Davis—Cookin': Prestige 7094 (1956)

Miles Davis—Relaxin': Prestige 7129 (1956)

Miles Davis And The Modern Jazz Giants: Prestige 7150 (1956)

Miles Davis—Workin': Prestige 7166 (1956)

Miles Davis Plays Jazz Classics: Prestige 7373 (1956)

Miles Davis—Steamin': Prestige 7580 (1956)

Miles Davis And John Coltrane Play Richard Rodgers: Prestige 7322 (1956/1958)

Sonny Rollins—Tenor Madness: Prestige 7657 (1956)

Leonard Bernstein—What Is Jazz?: Columbia 919 (1956)

Miles Davis—'Round About Midnight: Columbia 949 (1955/1956)

Four Tenor Saxes—Tenor conclave: Prestige 7249 (1956)

Paul Chambers—Whims of Chambers: Blue Note 1534 (1956)

Tadd Dameron—Mating Call: Prestige 7745 (1956)

Interplay For Two Trumpets And Two Tenors: Prestige 7341 (1957)

Johnny Griffin — A Blowing Session: Blue Note 1559 (1957)

Thelonious Monk With John Coltrane: Jazzland 46 (1957)

The Cats: New Jazz 8217 (1957)

Mal Waldron Sextet: Prestige 7341 (1957)

John Coltrane — Dakar: Prestige 7280 (1957)

John Coltrane — Paul Quinichette Quintet: Prestige 7158 (1957)

Coltrane Plays For Lovers: Prestige 7426 (1956 / 1957 / 1958)

John Coltrane — The First Trane: Prestige 7609 (1957)

John Coltrane — Lush Life: Prestige 7581 (1957 / 1958)

Thelonious Monk — Monk's Music: Riverside 3004 (1957)

John Coltrane — Traneing In: Prestige 7651 (1957)

John Coltrane — Blue Train: Blue Note 1577 (1957)

Prestige All Stars — Wheelin' And Dealin': Prestige 8327 (1957)

Sonny Clark — Sonny's Crib: Blue Note 1576 (1957)

Winners Circle: Bethlehem 6024 (1957)

Red Garland — All Morning Long: Prestige 7130 (1957)

Red Garland — Soul Junction: Prestige 7181 (1957)

Red Garland — High Pressure: Prestige 7209 (1957)

Red Garland — Dig It: Prestige 7229 (1957)

The Ray Draper Quintet Featuring John Coltrane: New Jazz 8228 (1957)

Art Blakey Big Band: Bethlehem 6027 (1957)

Gene Ammons And His All Stars — Groove Blues: Prestige 7201 (1958)

Gene Ammons And His All Stars — The Big Sound: Prestige 7132 (1958)

John Coltrane — The Believer: Prestige 7292 (1958)

John Coltrane — The Last Trane: Prestige 7378 (1957 / 1958)

John Coltrane—Soultrane: Prestige 7531 (1958)

Kenny Burrell—John Coltrane: New Jazz 8276 (1958)

Wilbur Harden Quintet: Savoy 12127 (1958)

John Coltrane—Trane's Reign: Prestige 7746 (1958)

Miles Davis—Milestones: Columbia 1193 (1958)

John Coltrane—Black Pearls: Prestige 7316 (1958)

Miles Davis—Jazz Track: Columbia 1268 (1958)

Michael Legrand—Legrand Jazz: Columbia 8079 (1958)

Miles Davis—Miles And Monk At Newport: Columbia 8978 (1958)

John Coltrane—Stardust: Prestige 7268 (1958)

John Coltrane—Standard Coltrane: Prestige 7243 (1958)

John Coltrane—Bahia: Prestige 7353 (1958)

Wilbur Harden—Jazz Way Out: Savoy 13004 (1958)

Wilbur Harden—Tanganyika Strut: Savoy 13005 (1958)

George Russell—New York N.Y.: Decca 9216 (1958)

John Coltrane—Coltrane Time: United Artists 5638 (1958)

Ray Draper—A Tuba Jazz: Jubilee 1090 (1958)

Bags And Trane: Atlantic 1368 (1959)

Cannonball Adderley Quintet In Chicago: Mercury 20449 (1959)

Miles Davis—Kind Of Blue: Columbia 8163 (1959)

John Coltrane—Giant Steps: Atlantic 1311 (1959)

John Coltrane—Coltrane Jazz: Atlantic 1354 (1959/1960)

Echoes Of An Era: Roulette RE-120 (1960)

John Coltrane And Don Cherry—The Avant-Garde: Atlantic 1451
   (1960)

John Coltrane—My Favorite Things: Atlantic 1361 (1960)

John Coltrane—Coltrane Plays The Blues: Atlantic 1382 (1960)

John Coltrane—Coltrane's Sound: Atlantic 1419 (1960)

John Coltrane—The Coltrane Legacy: Atlantic 1553 (1959/1960)

The Best Of John Coltrane: Atlantic 1541

The Art Of John Coltrane—The Atlantic Years: Atlantic 2-313

Miles Davis—Someday My Prince Will Come: Columbia 8456
    (1961)

John Coltrane—Africa/Brass: Impulse 6 (1961)

John Coltrane—Olé Coltrane: Atlantic 1373 (1961)

John Coltrane—Coltrane Live At The Village Vanguard:
    Impulse 10 (1961)

John Coltrane—The Other Village Vanguard Tapes: ABC Impulse
    AS -9325 (1961)

John Coltrane—Impressions: Impulse 42 (1961/1962)

John Coltrane Quartet: Impulse 203 (1961)

John Coltrane—Coltrane: Impulse 21 (1962)

John Coltrane—Ballads: Impulse 32 (1961/1962)

Duke Ellington And John Coltrane: Impulse 30 (1962)

John Coltrane With Johnny Hartman: Impulse 40 (1963)

The Definitive Jazz Scene: Impulse 9101-Volume 3 (1963)

Selflessness—John Coltrane: Impulse 9161 (1963/1965)

John Coltrane—Coltrane "Live At Birdland": Impulse 50 (1963)

John Coltrane—Crescent: Impulse 66 (1964)

John Coltrane—A Love Supreme: Impulse 77 (1964)

The John Coltrane Quartet Plays: Impulse 85 (1965)

The New Wave In Jazz: Impulse 90

John Coltrane—Kulu Sé Mama: Impulse 9106 (1965)

John Coltrane—Ascension: Impulse 95 (1965)

New Thing At Newport: Impulse 94 (1965)

John Coltrane—Transition: Impulse 9195 (1965)

John Coltrane—Sun Ship: Impulse 9211 (1965)

John Coltrane—First Meditations: ABC Impulse AS 9332 (1965)

John Coltrane—Infinity: Impulse 9225 (1965/1972)

John Coltrane—Live In Seattle: Impulse 9202-2 (1965)

John Coltrane—Om: Impulse 9140 (1965)

John Coltrane—Meditations: Impulse 9110 (1965)

John Coltrane—Cosmic Music: Impulse 9148 (1966)

John Coltrane—Live At The Village Vanguard Again: Impulse 9124
   (1966)

John Coltrane—Concert In Japan: Impulse 9246-2 (1966)

John Coltrane—Expression: Impulse 9120 (1967)

John Coltrane—Interstellar Space: Impulse 9277 (1967)

Index